FINANCIALLY
SECURE

FINANCIALLY SECURE

AN EASY-TO-FOLLOW
MONEY PROGRAM FOR WOMEN

DEBORAH
McNAUGHTON

THOMAS NELSON PUBLISHERS

A Division of Thomas Nelson, Inc.
www.ThomasNelson.com

Copyright © 2002 by Deborah McNaughton

Published in Nashville, Tennessee, by Thomas Nelson, Inc.

Library of Congress Cataloging-in-Publication Data

McNaughton, Deborah, 1950–
    Financially secure : an easy-to-follow money program for women / Deborah McNaughton.
        p. cm.
    ISBN 0-7852-6551-1 (pbk.)
    1. Women—Finance, Personal. 2. Finance, Personal. I.Title.
    HG179.M385 2002
    332.024'042—dc21   2001051212

Printed in the United States of America

01 02 03 04 05 PHX 5 4 3 2 1

DEDICATION

———

To my wonderful husband Hal, who stayed anchored when the financial storm came our way, and we were able to endure.

To my greatest joys, my three daughters Tiffany, Christy and Mindy, who always wear smiles and encourage their mom.

My three wonderful sons-in-law, Mike, Kyle and Mike.

And my extended treasures who bring me great joy, my five grandchildren, Austin, Alexis, Aaron, Caleb and Katie.

CONTENTS

——

WOMAN TO WOMAN

Being financially fit is as significant as being physically fit. Some of us are in good financial and physical shape, while others of us are trying to improve our current situation. We diet, exercise, try to gain control of our lives; the same holds true with our finances. We spend, we cut back, and we try to save and gain control of our money. It's overwhelming to know where to begin.

I know in my life, being a married woman and raising three daughters, the need to have financial security. Financial security is very important to women, and I can attest to the fact that when your finances are in disarray, there is no security and your life feels out of control.

Most of my married life, my husband and I were self–employed. You can't imagine what a roller-coaster ride that can be, especially in the real estate business where the economy so directly affects your livelihood.

I know what it's like to have a lot of money, and I know what it's like to barely get by. No one ever took the time to show my husband and me how to properly manage our finances. No financial experts ever contacted us when our real estate business was booming to show us how to invest our money. It was the blind leading the blind.

When we decided to sell our real estate franchise business, the country was in an economic downturn. Our assets had dropped, and we put the money we made into another business that didn't get off the ground. Our income had dropped 70 percent, but that didn't make the bills go away. As a matter of fact, none of the bill collectors felt sorry for us. We had approximately $300,000 of debt, most of which was from the business we no longer had. This figure may startle you, but it included all the interest that kept compounding and pushing the debt higher.

We made stupid choices and decisions, and we listened to the wrong advisers who nearly bankrupted us. Talk about being stressed! We wondered whether we could ever climb out of that mess without filing for bankruptcy. It took a great deal of thinking, planning, crying, and praying. I couldn't blame God for getting us into the predicament. We did it ourselves. My "jabberbox," you know the enemy of your mind that plants negative thoughts, constantly surfaced. Thoughts like "you're never going to get out of this" or "you're not smart enough to solve this." How many of you have an overworked jabberbox? I know how to overcome the enemy of my mind. And that is with knowledge.

With the business we had sold, we were always waiting for the "big deal." The big deal was going to bail us out of the situation. But guess what? The big deal never happened. Maybe you are looking for the big deal or person to bail you out. If you are, it's time to wake up! It's not going to happen. You will feel much better with yourself if you solve your own problems and money issues by doing it yourself rather than depending on someone else to bail you out.

I believe in prayer. If I hadn't continued praying about our situation, I don't believe I would have gotten through it. While God may not plant money trees in your backyard or drop money from the sky, he will give you ideas and direct you to specialists and advisers who can help you devise a plan to get your life back in order. But you have to do your part.

The turning point in our lives occurred when our youngest daughter, Mindy, had emergency brain surgery, and I'd let the insurance lapse (to save money). She almost died before the procedure. She was healthy one minute, then near death the next.

I feared for my daughter's life, and I was scared that the hospital would not give her the best care when the administrators realized we had no insurance. I was wrong. Not only did the hospital provide the best doctors and surgeons, but my daughter's surgery was a success. She had hydrocephalus, and there was a blockage in her ventricles causing fluid to build up. Her brain had swelled up, sending her into a coma. But God is good. After the doctors inserted a shunt into her brain to relieve the pressure, she began her recovery. Many miracles occurred during that year with Mindy—enough miracles to write another book.

Following that incident, Hal and I knew we had to make a major change in our lives, thinking, and profession. That was when we changed careers, and the "big dealitis" was cured. We sought outside help from experts and created a plan to pay off all our debts.

It took many years for us to come out on top, more than ten to be exact, but with our plan in place we were able to slowly work out payment schedules with our past creditors and pay things off without filing for bankruptcy. We were also able to start saving and investing. Our experience shows that with careful planning and strategies, you too can become financially secure.

My passion is to work with people because I see a need to educate them about different areas of finance. I have lived the good and the bad, and if there is any way to help an individual strengthen her financial position, I want to be that coach. I am not a financial planner nor do I pretend to be. That is why I surround myself with financial experts and advisers and have a referral base. However I do know how to coach an individual from the basics of handling credit and money to the ultimate place of financial security for the future. That is my passion for you.

You need faith, hope, and a plan. You need faith in God, and faith you can achieve whatever you go after with the right direction. You need hope that there is always a solution to any situation. Hope will keep you going. And you need a plan that will give you the direction you must take to make your journey successful.

WHAT WOMEN REALLY WANT TO KNOW

In today's world women generally live longer than men. In fact, one out of three women will live to be one hundred years old. That's scary, and all the more reason for you to be responsible for your financial future now, not later.

Studies show that 80 to 90 percent of women will be solely responsible for their finances at some point in their lives.

Women have more financial influence, more purchasing power, and more career opportunities than at any time in history. However, our greatest challenge may be to obtain financial security. Every woman wants to know that she will be taken care of financially.

OUR GOAL IS FINANCIAL FREEDOM

This book will address all women and walk each one through financial scenarios of all kinds. Whether you're married, single, divorced, widowed, or a college student, this book will give you a total program of being financially fit. Building your money and financial portfolio may hurt a bit as you begin, but as you learn all the ins and outs of the financial world, you will be empowered with strength.

You may be blessed with no money problems, or be debt free with money stashed away, but unclear about how to plan for your future.

You may be a single woman living from paycheck to paycheck. You may be overextended with your credit cards and find that it's getting harder and harder to pay your bills.

You may be a single mom raising your children alone and trying to stay afloat. Your dream is to own a home and find security, but you're not sure how to do it.

You may be recently divorced and have your credit report ruined because of your ex-husband. You're not sure how to get back on your feet and begin a new life. Maybe the divorce didn't leave you in dire straits, and you have a settlement that must be invested, but you haven't a clue about what to do.

You may be a college student who took advantage of specially targeted credit card offers, and now you need to know how to handle your credit card debt. Maybe you were never taught how to handle your finances at home or at school, and you don't want to make a mistake. You may even want to begin saving for your future. Where do you start?

You may be a widow with money to invest, but scared to take a chance. Or you may be a widow who was left with high debt and not enough money to make ends meet.

You may be a married woman in charge of paying the bills, and you just can't seem to make the budget work. Or maybe your husband is the one who pays the bills, and you don't know anything about your finances.

You may be retired, and need to know how to live on a set income.

This book will provide financial details you need to know about.

LET'S GET STARTED

I suggest you get a journal to write your thoughts and plans in. Call it your Financial Journal. You'll be surprised at how fast you progress and the success you'll achieve by journalizing your thoughts and plans about money.

To be successful in your finances you must follow all the steps outlined in this book from A through Z. You can't reach Z first. You have to work your way through from the beginning to the end to get where you want to be. There may be hurdles and obstacles in your way throughout this journey, but this book will hold your hand from the beginning to the end.

Now let's get started strengthening your financial position and making this journey one of growth. May you achieve financial security and inner peace as you implement what you read about here.

Before you turn to Chapter 1, take this short quiz to see where you are today with your money and finances. It will show you your strengths and weaknesses.

WORKOUT

Weigh In: Your Money Habits

Answer each of the following questions, and record your responses in your journal.

1. How often do you shop? Do you shop to fulfill emotional needs?

2. If a store offers you a discount for opening up a charge account, do you immediately apply? Do you rationalize this decision by telling yourself that you're getting a discount?

3. If you were to experience a sudden emergency, do you have any savings or assets set aside to get you through it?

4. If you're behind on your bill payments, do you wait until you get some money to pay them off, or do you contact your creditors and inform them of your situation?

5. Do you have any idea how much debt you owe? Have you ever calculated your debt to income ratio?

6. Do you and your spouse talk openly and often about your financial situation?

7. Is it common for you to pay one credit card bill by taking out a cash advance from another credit card?

8. Do you dream of a lump sum of money, such as winning the lottery, to drop into your lap and solve all your financial problems?

9. Do you pay off your account balances in full each and every month?

Review your answers. If you shop without a budget, apply for all kinds of credit cards, have no emergency funds, never communicate responsibly with your creditors, have no idea how much debt you have or even if you can afford it, never sit down and discuss finances with your spouse, juggle your credit card payments just to stay afloat, tell yourself you'll win the lottery and that'll take care of everything, and can't possibly pay off your account balances—well, you're in financial trouble.

1

How You Got into This Shape

Whatever financial shape you're in right now, it probably didn't happen overnight. Whether you are completely out of debt or on the edge of bankruptcy, it is the result of a pattern of financial management you have formed. The chocolate bars didn't make you do it. The great white sales didn't make you charge it. Nobody twisted your arm to charge and spend, and nobody forced you to be frugal and save.

The truth of the matter is that the way you act and handle your money is a direct result of what you learned or observed in your childhood. Now before you go after your mom and dad or guardians to thank them or scold them for this learned behavior, step back and analyze what you actually learned from them.

Were your parents or guardians good savers? Were they quick to pull out the credit cards? Were they always buying things to keep up with their friends? Did they shop impulsively? Who handled the money in your family? What happened to you when you asked for money? Was there ever a discussion about money in your home?

I would venture to guess that in most homes discussion of money and handling credit never occurred. If it did take place, it was probably in a vague way with no real teaching of money and credit management.

When I was growing up, my father gave my mother money to pay the bills and get things for the home and the family. Whenever I asked for money, I usually went to my mother first, then to my father. My father would make me practically beg for the money so that the thrill of getting it on those rare occasions was taken away. My father believed in paying cash for everything; he taught me to save for a rainy day and not to use credit.

Now, I can look back and see how as an early adult I was clueless about how to handle money. I started working in my father's grocery store when I was fourteen years old. With the money I made working, I seldom asked for money from my parents. It wasn't worth the battle.

After I was married I was excited to get our first line of credit for a Singer sewing machine. It didn't take long to pay off the sewing machine. Then came the department store credit card. I still remember the day I took that store card and had a field day. I charged several items and rushed home to show my husband, Hal. He took one look at my bundle of items and said, "How did you pay for it?" I was stunned. I quickly said, "I didn't have to pay for it. I charged it."

That piece of plastic seemed harmless at the time. No money slipped through my fingers, but reckoning day was to come. The bill arrived in no time. It was time to pay up. The minimum payments looked easy enough, so that's what I paid. Reality took a while to sink in. As a matter of fact, it took several years. I was trapped.

I felt liberated when I got my first credit card. I didn't have to ask anyone for permission to use it, and I got what I wanted when I wanted it. Yet I never really understood the importance of handling money and credit cards until my spending spun out of control.

Nobody ever taught me the proper way to handle money. The only thing I learned was what *not* to do. After all, who taught my parents about money? My parents were raised during the Depression when money was scarce, and they learned how to save. I grew up in a totally different generation, and we set out to spend, spend, spend.

Let's see how some other women were brought up. Each story will create a different situation that may relate to you.

MANDY'S STORY

Mandy had been married for five years and never knew how much was in the bank or what the family's financial situation really was. Her husband, Roy, paid the bills and gave Mandy an allowance to run the household.

Whenever Mandy asked Roy about their finances, he told her not to worry about it; he had everything under control. Mandy felt that she was in the dark, but she accepted Roy's answer. As long as she received her weekly allowance for the household, she was satisfied.

When Mandy was a child, she watched her father give her mother money every week to run their household, so she thought that was the proper way to handle money and finances in a marriage. Basically Mandy stuck her head in the sand. She was never taught differently.

KATHY'S STORY

When Kathy got married, she and her husband, Bill, decided that they were going to try to pay cash for things that they wanted and start saving at an early age.

Bill owned his business, so when things were good, there was always a positive cash flow of money to do just that.

After Bill and Kathy's two children were born, things got tighter with their finances. It wasn't long before they began using their credit cards as a convenience with the intention to pay off the balances each month. They had a small savings account set aside in case of an emergency, but not really the amount they had hoped to save.

Bill's business suddenly was hit with a weak economy, and the cash flow slowed down. The bills piled up. Kathy began handling the bills but was frustrated because Bill was unable to give her the money to pay them on time. Arguments broke out continuously. Bill would promise Kathy that there was a big order coming in that would end their money problems. It felt good for a while to hear those promises, but the reality was, nothing changed. Their dream of being debt free with money in the bank was altered. They spent all their savings trying to keep up with their bills.

When Kathy was growing up, her mother handled the bills. Many times she would hear her mother and father arguing over money and her mother crying.

There was never any discussion in her family about what exactly their money problems were, but Kathy decided that when she got married, there would be no fighting about money issues. Now here she was, repeating the same scenes she saw in her childhood home. The situation was more painful because she felt she had failed in her vow never to allow this to happen to her.

Bill's parents, on the other hand, had many lean times. Bill's father suddenly had a turn of events in his life that made him quite a bit of money. His parents' attitude was to splurge when the times were good, never putting that money away to grow. Bill saw only the good times and forgot about the lean times as he was growing up.

DANI'S STORY

Dani was single. She had a good job and made a nice income. She enjoyed the better things in life and took pride in the clothes she wore, the car she drove, and the friends she had.

While Dani was well accepted within her circle of friends, she always felt she needed to have the best in everything she bought. She would buy her friends gifts, pick up the tab when dining out with friends, and continuously lavish herself with material things. Dani was a compulsive shopper. She had outfits she never wore hanging in her closet with the price tags still on them.

She didn't save any money. Her attitude was, Why save for tomorrow when I can live for today?

When Dani was growing up, both parents were alcoholics. The money her parents brought home was spent on alcohol. Their house was a mess, and Dani's clothes came from secondhand stores. She was too embarrassed to bring her friends home, and she felt self-conscious about her clothing. Dani felt rejected and vowed to change her situation when she became an adult.

KAREN'S STORY

Karen had been married for thirty years when her husband died. He had always handled the finances and took care of all the decisions for their retirement.

When he passed away, he left Karen with quite a bit of money in different funds and accounts but never told her what to do with them. While going through the files for each account, Karen felt overwhelmed. She chastised herself for not being more actively involved with their investments.

Karen never took an interest in knowing their financial situation. She never wanted to face the fact that someday she would be alone, so it was easier not to learn.

As children, Karen's parents had gone through the Depression. They saved and saved, and when her father passed away, her mother was taken care of. Karen never heard her parents discuss retirement, but unbeknownst to Karen, her mother knew exactly what to do when her father died. Karen assumed that because she never heard her parents discussing their retirement, everything fell into place with no hitches when her father died. Boy, was she wrong.

ANALYZING THESE STORIES

Now let's go back and analyze each story.

Mandy definitely was following her mother and father's example. By not hearing her parents discuss finances and only observing money being given to her mother weekly, Mandy thought that was how marriage was supposed to be. She felt guilty questioning her husband, Roy. It was easier for her to walk away from any involvement with the finances than make Roy upset by questioning him. As long as she felt secure for the moment, there was no reason to upset her husband. She didn't worry about the future as long as she got her weekly allowance.

This is a dangerous situation. If anything ever happened to Roy, Mandy would have no clue about their financial situation. She definitely needed to make changes so she would not have a false sense of security.

Kathy had great intentions about planning for her and Bill's future. You could see how she would be determined not to replay the hard times she saw her parents go through. With Bill's background of always depending on the big deal to make money, Kathy was on a roller coaster. One minute things were good; the next minute they were bad.

Kathy needed to be more involved with Bill's business and look at the whole picture rather than the one big deal that would bail them out of their financial mess. Instead of being consumed with guilt by not wanting money problems like those of her parents, she could help Bill focus on living for today and paying the bills rather than the future of the big deal that may never happen.

Dani's situation is quite obvious. With her childhood being out of control, you can see why she felt she needed to always be in control through her compulsive shopping and spending. Needing to feel accepted by her peers was important to her. Dani felt that by lavishing herself and her friends with material things, she would not be rejected.

Dani must get control of her situation and learn that she can control her life and finances. She needs to look out for herself not only for today but also for her future.

Karen had a great life until her husband died. She took a risk by not asking her mother how she was making it after her father died. Assuming that everything just falls into place when a spouse dies is once again false security.

Whether you are married or single, there comes a point in your life that you must not focus only on how your parents managed their money. You have to come to terms with your own situation and take action with your finances.

Schools very seldom educate students on the subject of money and finances. If the schools don't teach money management, and our parents don't teach us properly, we will learn the hard way.

As an adult you must try to reflect on your childhood money and financial training. Is it helping you now or causing you distress in managing your money? It's time to grow up and take charge of your destiny.

CHILDHOOD MONEY MEMORIES

As you've learned from the stories here, we tend to get our financial patterns from our families. We may not realize that we pick up our "money traditions" from childhood, but we do. This doesn't mean that you're doomed to repeat what you observed growing up. You can take control of your financial destiny. But it's a good idea for you to travel back in time and think about what you saw or heard (or didn't see or hear) and then reflect on your financial habits. Who were your role models? What kinds of emotions arise when you think about money, bills, and your future?

WRAP-UP

All of this information will help you understand how you deal with your finances. Once you have some sense of where you came from, then you'll be able to create new financial habits that will help you make your way to financial security.

COACH'S TIP

Be patient with yourself as you work through this book. Do not expect overnight miracles. Do believe in yourself. Do believe in taking small, consistent steps over a period of time. Do set realistic goals. If you experience a setback, don't give up! Learn from it, and continue working on your financial fitness.

2

OVERCOMING YOUR GREATEST FEARS

Most of us have fears about money. It seems that no matter how hard we try, there's just never enough of it to go around. Are you fearful and intimidated by your financial situation? If you answered yes, then rest assured, you are not alone. The best way to overcome fear is to do the very thing you fear the most. In this case the best way to get rid of financial stress is to learn money management for yourself. Then pass this knowledge on to some of your friends, family, and children. Let them learn from your wealth of financial knowledge.

Money fears come in different shapes and sizes. Open your journal and review some of the entries you've made. What are some of your money fears and anxieties? On a separate piece of paper, briefly list them. Now go through your childhood experiences. Can you see any cause or root that explains your fear or anxiety, maybe even some of your spending habits? Don't worry if you can't find a specific cause for each fear. Chances are, as you continue to read this book, you'll uncover many answers and solutions that will enhance your financial security.

KELLY'S STORY

I was being interviewed on a talk radio program when Kelly phoned in. She'd already filed two bankruptcies and wanted to know how she could get back on track without repeating her past mistakes. Kelly was afraid that her old spending habits would cause her to end up in another bankruptcy.

The first thing I asked Kelly was, "When you were young and living at home, did you typically have to beg your parents for money to get something that you really wanted?" She answered, "Yes."

I then asked, "When you left home and received your first credit cards, did you feel empowered?" Again she answered, "Yes." Free from having to beg for money, Kelly felt that she could now buy whatever she wanted. That made her feel good—until the bills became higher than her income.

Once Kelly realized that her problem was a result of being in charge of her own money, she realized how out of control she was. That was Kelly's first step. The next step was to learn how to be responsible with her money and credit, and consequently abstain from recklessly spending her money.

FEAR OF NOT SAVING ENOUGH

Do you worry because you're not saving any money? Many women go through life without ever setting aside money for a rainy day or retirement. Sometimes we put it off because we think we don't have the "extra" money to do so. You might be waiting for a magical raise that will give you the extra boost to finally start stashing your cash away. You may even be secretly relying upon a fiscally savvy Prince Charming to come along to save you. Whatever your current reasoning, it's time to change how you think right now. You can't afford to wait until someday arrives to start saving.

Here's where you transform an old money belief into a new one. Don't view savings as an extra. Instead think of savings as paying yourself. If it helps, think of savings as a bill you owe to yourself. Your savings, aka your hard-earned dollars, will give you money for tomorrow, next year, that sudden emergency, and your retirement years. Even if you have yet to save a dime, you can start doing so immediately. If you can spare only a few dollars a week, then start there. If you can afford more, even better.

The trick is to take action. You can have your company or bank subtract a specified amount from each pay period's check. You can pretend that the amount you put in savings doesn't exist for you to spend. Whatever you need to do to convince yourself to save money, do it. One day, you'll be pleasantly surprised by how much your savings have grown and how you no longer worry about not saving.

LIVING FROM PAYCHECK TO PAYCHECK

If you're barely making it from paycheck to paycheck, are over-extended on your credit, and are not paying off all of your monthly bills, you have serious cause to be concerned. Most likely you are already stressed out and scared that one emergency will send you over the edge. The truth is, you are absolutely right to be concerned. But before you beat yourself up, pat yourself on the back because the fact that you're reading this book means you've sought help. Next, ready yourself to do battle. It's going to take some focus and some time, but you can get your finances under control.

The most important thing to do is to get a grip on your immediate essential finances. Savings will have to come later. By taking immediate action, you'll lose some of your anxiety. Once you see what you can achieve by managing the essentials, you'll have the confidence to begin saving for your future.

WORRIED ABOUT YOUR FINANCIAL FUTURE?

Maybe you've managed to set some money aside, but will it be enough for retirement? As much as I hate to say it, you're right to worry. In general, women save less than men. One factor is that women tend to make less than men. If you take time off to be a stay-at-home mom, you lose Social Security work credits, resulting in lower pension payments. Another factor is that women save for more immediate things such as trips, clothes, and household items.

I don't want to sound too bleak, but here are some facts for you to consider:

- 22 percent of women never marry.

- 52 percent of marriages end in divorce.

- 75 percent of women outlive their spouses.

- In 64 percent of single-parent households, women are the providers.

Rather than let this information intimidate us, we're going to focus on learning what it takes to plan for our future. The only way to address this fear is to realize that we have a terrific need to prepare ourselves and not rely or depend upon someone else for our own financial future. Are you ready for the challenge? The training you need is contained within this book, so read on.

FEAR OF MISHANDLING CREDIT

Some women may be new to credit and fear they may go overboard with it. You may have heard the war stories of family and friends and wonder, *How does that happen?* Well, have you ever found yourself thinking, *I work hard, so what if I treat myself to a little something*? This isn't such a bad thought, right? How could all those persuasive ads—you know, the ones telling you how life would be a dream if only you had this or that—possibly be wrong? So you use your credit card, which lets you have that far-off dream today. And that's how it starts. When you rely upon tomorrow to pay for today's expenses, you're living beyond your means. You are in denial of your current situation, which, more often than not, signals financial trouble ahead.

ARE YOU AN OVERSPENDER?

1. Are you presently making only minimum payments on a large balance?

2. If so, are you still using that credit card to make even more purchases that you can't pay off?

3. Do you use one credit card to pay off another?

4. Do you lie or try to hide your credit card purchases from loved ones?

5. Are you behind or delinquent in your payments?

6. Do you use more than one credit card and run up balances greater than what you can afford to pay off each month?

7. Do you live in fear of creditors?

8. Do you make large purchases before spending any time thinking about them?

9. If you had the choice to pay with cash or a credit card, is your first choice a credit card?

10. Are you counting on winning the lottery to pay off your bills?

If you answered yes to more than two questions, you have a problem. The time has come for you to stop overspending.

CREDIT CONTROL

Most problems arise with credit cards. Yes, I know that colorful plastic card feels more like play money than cold, hard-earned cash, but it isn't! Using your credit card to make purchases that you don't have cash for is the surest way to get into debt. But with knowledge and a handy calculator, you can put yourself on a healthy spending track—and keep yourself there.

Whenever you use your credit card, keep a registry of each purchase. Use an index card or some type of tracking system, such as your checkbook registry, that you can put into your purse or wallet. Review these amounts, and then set a monthly limit. This limit should be an amount you can comfortably pay off in full each month. For example, if you charge $300 and know that's all you can pay off that month, stop charging. By doing this, you are in control of your credit card use.

EMOTIONS AND SHOPPING

Bored or depressed? Is life lacking some luster? Fleeing the doldrums of life is another reason people overspend. It's fun and easy to pretend to be a big spender, carelessly buying items that you think will make you feel good—that is, until the bills come. Many people try to relieve depression or boredom with a dose of shopping. Do you make dates with your girlfriends to meet and spend a day at the mall? A lot of us do. Shopping is a deeply entrenched social aspect of our culture, especially female culture. But at what cost do you find happiness?

Think about all those advertisements and the toll they take on your mind. Buy and be happy! Or will you? Unfortunately the afterglow of most purchases fades quickly. The funny thing is, once it's gone, most of us will head right back out to shop some more. You may think, *Oh, well, if I'm not personally fulfilled, at least others will look at me and think I am!* Except you're the one left holding the bill.

DON'T FALL FOR THE ENTICEMENTS

To make matters worse, most department stores offer discount incentives to get you to sign up for their in-house credit cards. Ten percent off your first purchase may sound good. But let's do some number crunching. You purchase some cute clothes for $120. Ten percent of $120 equals savings of $12. Wow! So now you're paying $108. What a deal! Which is exactly what the stores want you to think. They count on you to focus on that $12 rather than the $108 you actually spent. If they've enticed you into their little trap and convinced you to sign up for their credit cards, guess what? You lose.

Credit card companies as well as department stores know how to hit your weaknesses. The credit card company knows that most individuals who open an account for a discount will not pay the balance in full when the statement arrives. Most department store charge cards have an interest rate between 20 and 22 percent. If you don't pay the balance in full when the statement is due, the 10 percent you saved is lost to the high interest rate you'll be paying by making only minimum payments. Remember, creditors are in the business of taking money from you. Don't let them outsmart you. Don't fall prey to their trap! Don't charge! Pay cash!

IMPULSE BUYING

Then there's the impulse purchase. Retail stores are designed to entice you with their products. They arrange every inch of their stores with the idea of getting you to make a purchase. Don't believe me? The next time you are standing in line at the checkout counter, notice all of the inexpensive items of nail polish, accessories, cosmetics, and so on. They come in all kinds of different colors. *Why not?* you think. *They're so cheap, I'll buy two.* Impulsively you add these items to your purchase. Again, the retailer comes out on top because he has just succeeded in increasing the sale. Oops! The retailer won again. The lesson? Think twice before you buy.

PREVENTING CREDIT AND MONEY PROBLEMS

The best way to handle credit and money issues is to prevent problems before they happen. Most people can afford to pay only 10 percent of their net income to installment debt, not including mortgage payments. Surprised by that figure? It's not a lot. If you're paying more than 15 percent to installment debt, it's time to cut back. And if you pay 20 percent or more? Stop. You are in financial trouble and should cease using credit right now. More than 25 percent—that's really bad news. You may need professional help as well as a drastically different and more financially sound lifestyle.

Next, credit grantors estimate your net income, figuring 80 percent of your gross income (before taxes). Living expenses, such as rent and bills, shouldn't exceed 70 percent of your income, while variable expenses, such as food, fuel, utilities, and so forth, are calculated between 15 and 25 percent. Credit grantors prefer that only 90 to 95 percent of your net income be committed to all expenses. If they find you exceed these numbers, chances are, you're probably overextended on credit.

DEBT TO INCOME RATIO

Are these percentages overwhelming you? Don't worry. You needn't be a rocket scientist to figure out these numbers. You can determine your debt to income ratio by using the following very simple formula. With your calculator in hand, take your monthly net income (after taxes) and divide it by your total monthly debt. The result is your percentage of debt.

Your total monthly debt divided by your net monthly income equals your debt ratio.

Remember that 10 percent is where you want to be, 15 percent is fair, and anything over that signals financial trouble.

It's easiest to avoid financial trouble by handling credit problems before they start. How? Limit the number of credit cards you carry to three, reserving $1,000 to $2,000 of unused credit for emergencies. Should you need some incentive, know that unused credit can cause problems when applying for a home or automobile loan. If the credit grantor factors unused credit into the estimate, this will raise your debt ratio.

Pay cash for small purchases, because you want to avoid paying interest for an extended period of time on items with fleeting value. When you need to make a big credit purchase, analyze how much it's really going to cost you. Never make a decision at a lender's office. Opt to go home and sleep on it instead. You work hard for your money, so learn to spend it wisely.

WRAP-UP

Are you able to breathe just a little bit easier now that you've learned how to take control of your fears and concerns about money and credit management? I know it's tough to look at such things directly. But if things are to get better, you must face your fears. Remind yourself that fear is simply negative faith and that you are truly capable of handling your own money. Come up with a plan. Doing so gives you the advantage you need to become financially successful. And the sooner you take action, the better you'll feel.

You can change the money beliefs you've previously held. These beliefs are simply that, *beliefs*. They are external to you. Learn to believe in your new financial habits, practice them, and see where they take you. If you follow all the steps provided in this book, you'll end up financially sound and worry free.

COACH'S TIP

Still feeling overwhelmed by your fears and old money habits? Can't seem to work your way out of debt on your own? Get more help! Debtors Anonymous is a nationwide support program for people with spending problems. Write Debtors Anonymous, General Services Board, P.O. Box 92088, Needham, Massachusetts 02492-0009, or call (781) 453-2743. The Website is www.New@DebtorsAnonymous.org.

3

LET'S TALK

———

Talking about personal money issues is considered taboo. Most
women have a hard time sharing their problems or concerns
about money and financial issues with other people.

Yet all of us, at some time or another, must learn about finances.
Too many of us learn the hard way. It's far easier to get information,
and to address your fears, by talking to someone about your situation. When you do open up to others you may discover that they've
experienced a similar situation. Thus, they identify with your feelings and circumstances. Frequently they can give you solid advice
on how to deal with the situation or where to get help. And by networking with other women, you have the added benefit of emotional support.

MONEY TALK

Discussing your finances doesn't mean revealing your yearly income
or the dollar amount in your checking account. It means asking
questions, outlining scenarios, setting goals, reading up on topics
that interest you, surfing the Net, talking with friends, and availing

yourself of professional financial advice. Doing this helps you deal with the money you now have planned for your future.

Managing your money takes time and effort. Whether you're currently trying to get out of debt or preparing for your retirement, you must be consistently proactive with your planning. Since personal finance is a never-ending experience, expect to revisit your plans and reevaluate your goals. As your situation changes, you can revise both to suit your needs. That's why speaking up, networking, and getting the answers you need can be critical to attaining the financial advantage.

GETTING ADVICE

A number of financial specialists can help you take control of your money:

- Accountants can assist you with bookkeeping and help you file yearly taxes.

- Tax specialists can help you with tax problems or back payments to the IRS.

- Attorneys give you legal advice in areas such as wills, estate planning, and bankruptcy.

- Debt management companies can assist you with getting yourself out of debt.

- Debtors Anonymous is a nationwide support program for over-spenders.

- Financial brokers or investment representatives can help you with financial analysis as well as assist you with investment recommendations.

Use discretion when consulting with professionals. Ask for referrals from someone you trust, or check their credentials. And make sure you feel comfortable working with them.

BREAKING WITH THE PAST

Are you still feeling awkward breaking the code of financial silence? Then let's stop and think about why talking about money is such a big deal for you. Our society once taught that men handled the finances. Women weren't supposed to be openly concerned with money, even if they had to live with the repercussions of a father's, brother's, or husband's financial decisions. Money matters were private and not to be aired in public. And even though I'm sure there were instances where some women disregarded these social guidelines, women generally left finances to the men.

TIMES HAVE CHANGED

But our society has drastically changed. Increasingly women need to know how to manage their money, and one way they can do this safely is by networking. Consider this:

- In 75 percent of all households, women possess equal say in financial matters.

- By the year 2005, women are expected to make up approximately 62 percent of the workforce.

It is definitely no longer wise or feasible to stick our heads in the sand, pretending that we can't or don't need money skills for ourselves. If these statistics aren't impressive enough, did you know that women own 50 percent of small businesses? That's approximately 9.1 million women!

WOMEN AND INVESTING

Consequently women are turning to investments as a means to attain their financial and lifestyle goals, and they are approaching these goals via investment firms and investment clubs. This interest has, in turn, captured the attention of the consumer market, which is just beginning to realize that women want information regarding personal finance. In trying to address these needs, recent marketing studies have found that a lot of women are intimidated by some of the older, more formal methods that traditional brokerage and financial management firms observe.

The good news is these businesses are responding by learning more about how to connect with women and becoming more attuned to their needs. Having focused more exclusively on men in the past, these firms are actively seeking to gain the loyalty and business of female clients.

WOMEN AND FINANCES:
THE WAVE OF THE FUTURE

Some marketing experts believe that the combination of women and finances will be a powerful trend in the very near future. As women create more wealth and join the workforce in larger numbers, the greater their interest in protecting and growing that wealth. Add retirement concerns and how to plan for them into the mix, and it's easy to see why women are seeking financial advice.

Due to the nature of our current society, women may be slowing down to look at the big picture and ultimately discovering what really, truly matters to them: financial security. That raises the questions: What kind of life do you want to have? What about your future? And how can you achieve these goals? Engaging the professional services of an investment firm that can help you set up a financial plan for your future is a tried and practical way to get the assistance you need.

Check out these resources:

- American Business Women's Association
- Organization for Investment Clubs
- Chamber of Commerce
- The Institute of Certified Financial Planners

Or visit financial Web sites geared specifically to women:

- Women's Financial Network (www.wfn.com)
- www.financialmuse.com
- www.msmoney.com

The bottom line: even a substantial number of married women are setting goals and taking control of their own finances. Don't miss out on being one of them just because you feel you don't know enough. There are plenty of ways to get help and to improve your situation!

WRAP-UP

After reading all of this, I hope you've become inspired to talk about money issues. Dealing with your money directly can be an exhilarating process. Knowledge really is the key to gaining the financial advantage, along with consistent and sound money practices. Once you've looked at all the options, implement money management and start saving—these are your greatest training tools! After your system is in place, you'll derive satisfaction from knowing that you can manage your money and plan for your future. So I encourage you: discuss your money concerns, network, and seek financial help. Just be sure to use your discretion and work with reputable advisers, firms, and organizations.

COACH'S TIP

Don't forget to see the silver lining surrounding your financial circumstances. No matter what state they're in, the opportunity is there for you to make them better. Use this time to think about what you want. Ask yourself, *What really matters to me?* Once you know the answer to that question, target that area and focus your energies on it. It is your road map to financial change.

4

IGNORANCE IS NOT BLISS

There may be a time in your life when you face a financial situation that will cause you great distress. It may be an unforeseen emergency, a sudden illness, or the loss of a job. Caught unawares, you do your best to keep your finances in line. Yet in spite of all your efforts, you may fall behind on all your monthly obligations.

Financial hardship is an extremely trying and stressful experience. It's a time when your jabberbox, the enemy of your mind, will work overtime, causing you fear and anxiety by constantly reminding you of all the what-ifs. Not having enough money to cover your expenses can make you feel scared, ashamed, depressed, and helpless. It can cause you to lose sleep at night.

You may retreat from friends and family because you feel embarrassed by your situation. Or you may try to ignore the problem, hoping and praying that this financial disaster will just disappear. Denial is a common way to handle financial stress. On the other hand you may be constantly preoccupied with your outstanding debt, living in constant fear of the repercussions that will result.

Your work will be affected by this stress, and marital problems may arise. How will you ever manage to juggle all of your payments and get back on your feet again?

The worst thing you can do is nothing! Force yourself to stand up straight and tall, and then take action. Action will produce the results you need. Remember, knowledge brings power; power brings action.

FACING CREDIT PROBLEMS

First, let's deal with what's upsetting you. Sit down, take a deep breath, and gather your thoughts together. Now make a list of your worries and fears; keep this list in your journal. Are you anxious that you're unable to pay a bill on time? Troubling as this may be, how critical is this one event in comparison to losing your life, your health, your family, your faith, or your friends? This is a reminder to think of the big picture and to put things in the right perspective. Not being able to pay your bills isn't life threatening. Yes, you may lose sleep over it, and your credit report may be ruined, but at least you still have the support of your loved ones. And although it may take time, you will eventually put things back in order and get on your feet again.

Now that you've gained some perspective, it's time to take action. Knowing your options is critical. This knowledge will help you prepare to face your creditors and the collection agencies. Figure out how much you do have. Then, identify your priorities. Think in terms of what it will take for you to survive. Housing, utilities, food, a telephone—all of these things are essential. Next, determine which bills need to be paid off immediately. Consider the consequences involved with each bill and the degree of severity if you don't pay it on time. Finally, formulate a plan. Be realistic about what you can do. Don't try to do too much. Most important, don't offer payment on something you can't make good on.

CHERYL'S STORY

Cheryl was a single woman who'd been laid off her job. She'd been earning a large salary and had a good savings account, and she felt that being laid off would be a temporary setback until she got another job.

As the weeks and months went by, finding another job seemed like an impossible task. Everywhere she turned, interviewers told her she was overqualified for the job. Cheryl's savings account was slowly diminishing. Her bills were getting further and further behind. The creditors were calling her daily, demanding to know when her next payment was coming. Things escalated, until they got so bad she refused to take their calls.

One creditor in particular was calling several times a day and threatening her. Although he was an employee of a department store, the caller was using the tactics of an outside collection company. Cheryl was so stressed out that she couldn't concentrate, sleep, or eat. She was living in fear.

Cheryl contacted me about her problem with the department store creditor. She told me about the threats, and I suggested she file a complaint with the Federal Trade Commission (FTC). She had tapes of messages the creditor had left along with notes specifying the dates and times of her conversations with this particular individual.

Upon receipt of her complaint, the FTC began to investigate this company. The agency's representatives contacted Cheryl to get more information. She found out that there had been numerous complaints besides her own involving this company and that it was undergoing further investigation.

Needless to say, the harassing phone calls finally stopped. And Cheryl realized the importance of taking the necessary steps to stop the harassment.

Most people don't know their legal rights or the proper agency to contact to file a complaint in this situation. Again, knowledge is your best tool. Know your legal rights and the actions you can take when dealing with a harassing creditor.

CONTACTING YOUR CREDITORS

You've devised a plan for what you are able to pay; now it's time to notify all your creditors of your situation. Don't make the mistake of thinking, *Things will get better shortly, so why let them know?* Waiting until your payments are overdue is simply not the way to go; communicating is. You can contact each creditor with a phone call or a letter. Initially you may want to call because it's a quicker method. However, it's probably a good idea to follow up with a letter, because then you'll have a paper trail showing all your interactions with the company. Keep copies of correspondence in your files. Always send a letter by certified mail with a return receipt.

In your letter you should include the following information: the date; the appropriate address; the account number; and the correct department/person in charge. In the body of the letter, restrict yourself to stating basic information. If you're following up a phone agreement, stick with your payment offer. Ask the creditor for a written response to your letter, and sign your name.

Don't expect your creditors to be sympathetic to your situation. They're in the business of collecting money, and they've heard every story in the book. Don't take it personally. You're only a name on their computer screen. They don't know you. On the flip side, your honesty and responsibility may make them more willing to work with you because they didn't have to track you down.

Communicating with your creditors may not be the most pleasant thing you've ever done, but ultimately it will make you feel better because you're taking some form of action, relieving you of some stress.

NEGOTIATING WITH CREDITORS

Once you've informed your creditors of your circumstances, offer a solution based upon your plan. Let them know that your situation is temporary. If you can pay a reduced amount, tell them that. It may take some work on your part, but having an amount or payment plan that you can stick to may be the best approach under these circumstances.

If you feel that you can't negotiate over the phone, ask a family member or a friend to do it for you. If you're seriously in debt, contact a debt management company to help you set reasonable payments. The firm can act as your go-between with the creditors. In some instances you may have to consider hiring an attorney.

No matter which approach you take, stay calm. Focus on your goal, which is to negotiate a plan that works for you. Do not be swayed by creditors' requests for immediate or bigger payments. Their job is to bring the account up to date, so they will try any means available to do so. Keep that in mind as you stick to your plan.

SAMPLE LETTER TO A CREDITOR

October 25, 20–

AXPB Inc.

1222 Main St.

Yourtown, NY 88888

Account number: 129586069

Dear Customer Service,

I have recently been laid off from my job. I would like to pay you $20 per month until I return to work. At that time, I will contact you to make payment arrangements so that I can bring my account up to date.

If this is acceptable to you, please respond in writing.

Sincerely,

Anne Smith

COMMON STRATEGIES

The most common negotiation tactic is to ask for a payment reduction. Tell the creditors that when you're able to, you'll increase the payment, but right now the amount you're offering is the best you can do. Be persistent, and see if they'll accept a lower monthly payment. For example, if your payments are $80 a month, reduce them to $40 a month. Just make sure that you really can make this payment and be on time with it.

Another approach is to extend the payment period. This tactic may work, but it depends upon the type of loan or credit you're dealing with. For instance, if you're trying to pay off an item with a set term, such as a car or a computer, on a twenty-four-month contract, suggest twenty-seven months. Or offer an "interest only" payment until you're back on your feet again.

Remember! It's in your best interest to see what you can work out with creditors. The only way to find out what they'll accept is to contact them and make your offer. If they accept it verbally on the phone, ask them to put it in writing and mail it to you. Don't make a payment until you receive the letter of agreement. Creditors frequently have short memories without letters of confirmation.

What happens if you've contacted your creditors and they've accepted your plan, but now you find that you can't hold up your end of the deal? Again, don't avoid communicating with them. As soon as you realize you can't follow through with the agreed payment, contact them. Let them know that you overestimated what you could pay. But be prepared to follow up with another plan. Give them an amount that you can pay. And make the payment in a timely manner.

DEALING WITH COLLECTION AGENCIES

MARLENE'S STORY

Marlene called my debt counseling office in a panic. A collection agency had been continuously calling her at work, making threats that it would have her wages garnished if she didn't pay her bill immediately.

However, Marlene was unable to pay the bill. She had already told the collection agency that she didn't have the money, but that didn't stop the calls and letters. Her work was becoming affected by the harassment, and she couldn't sleep at night.

After Marlene explained her situation to me, I instructed her to tell the collection agency that she could not receive personal calls at her place of employment. I also informed her that nobody could garnish her wages unless there was a court judgment. In other words she would have to be sued by the creditor, and the creditor would have to win a court judgment to collect the money. There had been no lawsuit or judgment.

Marlene needed to formulate a plan when she had the finances to repay this debt, but until then nothing could be done.

Because of the abusive things that the collection agency told her, she thought that she would go to jail. Night after night, the fear of jail haunted her. When she expressed her fears, I informed her that there was no debtors' prison, and she needed to empower herself by learning what the Fair Debt Collection Practices Act stated so she could protect herself.

COLLECTION AGENCY TACTICS

A collection agency is contracted by a creditor to collect a debt. Usually the creditor has abandoned hope of getting the amount from you and turns the collection efforts over to an outside agency. For its efforts the collection agency will receive a percentage of the amount owed. Collection agencies are infamous for their tactics to get you to pay up. It's probably helpful to know that they're trained to intimidate you. Essentially it's their job to be ruthless, so prepare yourself for the worst.

WHAT YOU SHOULD KNOW

The Fair Debt Collection Practices Act was created to protect consumers from being unduly harassed by collection agencies. The act pertains to outside collection agencies and not the original creditors. Basically the act states,

- You cannot be called before 8:00 A.M.
- You cannot be called after 9:00 P.M.
- Agencies cannot call you so frequently that it can be interpreted as a form of harassment.
- Obscene language may not be used against you.
- Threats cannot be made against you.
- They cannot call you at work if your employer doesn't allow these types of calls.
- They cannot call you directly if you've hired an attorney to represent you.
- They cannot call family, friends, neighbors, or coworkers and inform them of your situation.

HANDLING ACCOUNTS THAT
GO INTO COLLECTION

If your account goes to a collection agency, you'll receive a letter from the agency. Review it carefully, looking for the name of the original creditor and the specific amount owed. The letter should also state that you have thirty days to dispute the validity of the debt. Make sure that the debt is yours and that it's for the proper amount. If there's an error, then dispute the debt. You may want to request verification regardless of whether you dispute the amount. Doing this may buy you some time, maybe even a couple of months, in terms of having to repay the debt. The agency should respond to your request by sending you verification of the debt.

A creditor that is not successful with one collection agency may opt to move the account to another collection agency. If this occurs, the new collection agency will contact you. Definitely request verification of the debt. It is not unusual when the account is passed around from one collection agency to another that the original information about your account becomes lost. This could be to your advantage when seeking verification, since the collection agency must respond. If the collection agency does not respond, it cannot try to collect the debt.

Phone conversations with collectors are never easy. Inform them of your situation, but don't give away more information than you need to. Know before you speak with them the amount you can pay. Be definite about this amount. Don't expect them to accept your offer right off the bat. Typically collectors will try to get the entire amount from you. They will try to pressure you, so be prepared to withstand this. It will probably take several failed attempts before the agency will even consider your offer.

If you are unable to make any payments, contact the collection agency, and let the collector know this. It may seem futile, but doing so may delay the agency's pursuit of a lawsuit or further collection efforts. Follow up any phone conversation with a letter, recapping the verbal agreement. Keep a copy of all correspondence for your files. When you talk to the collection agency, it's also a good idea to include a line that asks the agency to put this letter in your file. Send the letter by certified mail, and keep the return receipt.

You can elect to hire a debt management company or a lawyer who will deal with the collection agency. A payment arrangement or a one-time settlement may be something that someone other than you may be able to negotiate. Before you hire a lawyer, calculate whether the amount of the debt merits the amount you'll pay the lawyer. Lawyers' fees can be high. For a bill of few hundred dollars, you may be better off handling your own negotiations or going to a debt management company.

If the matter involves an actual item that you purchased on credit, you can offer to return the item. If the agency gets the creditor's approval, ask for a letter stating that upon receipt of the item, the debt will be considered paid in full. Also ask that the letter clearly state that a deficiency judgment will not be filed. If the agency won't accept this offer, you may want to sell the item to pay off the debt.

Collection agencies are persistent—be it through letters or phone calls. Their chances of collecting the debt are higher if they can reach you within three months of the account's becoming delinquent. Their chances diminish as the delinquent debt gets older.

NEGOTIATING WITH COLLECTION AGENCIES

Collection agencies follow guidelines established by the creditor that hired them. These guidelines are very specific. Whether settlement is full or partial, the creditor must approve the deal.

This is where your plan comes in: you've evaluated your situation, taken care of essentials, and figured out a realistic settlement or payment plan. You can expect the collection agency to exert pressure on you to pay off the entire amount or to increase the amount you're offering. The collector may counter with an offer, telling you that if you pay off the entire amount, you'll receive a 20 percent discount. This is another tactic to get you to immediately pay off as much of the debt as possible. Knowing this beforehand will help you stay calm and stick with your own plan.

TACTICS

There are two standard ways to approach a negotiation with a collection agency. One is to offer a lump sum, either the full amount or a lesser amount. Again, the creditor will have to approve this offer. Each creditor will have different policies. If you can, offer one-third or more of the amount owed in exchange for a cancellation of the debt. Some agencies will accept 50 percent of the amount, while others will take 60 percent to 80 percent.

When you present your offer, let the collector know it's final, and you want this offer to be considered payment in full. Also tell the collector that you want the debt removed from your credit report. If the collection agency agrees to your offer, request and receive a written confirmation of the settlement before you send in the payment. When you receive this letter, send in your payment shortly thereafter.

The best time for negotiations is the end of the month. That is when the creditor is trying to close its books out. The more accounts closed for the month, the better it looks on the records, so the creditor may be more amenable to your plan.

Another approach is to negotiate a payment plan. Most agencies will not decrease the amount owed in these situations. The reasoning is that generally people will stop making payments after the first two months or so. This forces the agency to increase the collection efforts (and the collector will follow through with additional attempts).

It really is best to make your payments until you pay off the amount owed. Prior to your last payment, you'll want to request that the agency send you a letter stating that once the balance is collected in full, the entry will be removed from your credit report. Do this before you mail in the last payment; otherwise, you'll lose the leverage you have with the agency.

STATUTE OF LIMITATIONS

If you owe money to a creditor, there is a limit to the amount of time the creditor can enforce for collection without the creditor suing you. As of 2001, here are the time limits:

Alabama	3 years	Montana	5 years
Alaska	6 years	Nebraska	4 years
Arizona	3 years	Nevada	4 years
Arkansas	3 years	New Hampshire	3 years
California	4 years	New Jersey	6 years
Colorado	6 years	New Mexico	4 years
Connecticut	6 years	New York	6 years
Delaware	3 years	North Carolina	3 years
District of Columbia	3 years	North Dakota	6 years
Florida	4 years	Ohio	6 years
Georgia	4 years	Oklahoma	3 years
Hawaii	6 years	Oregon	6 years
Idaho	4 years	Pennsylvania	6 years
Illinois	5 years	Rhode Island	10 years
Indiana	6 years	South Carolina	3 years
Iowa	5 years	South Dakota	6 years
Kansas	3 years	Tennessee	6 years
Kentucky	5 years	Texas	4 years
Louisiana	3 years	Utah	4 years
Maine	6 years	Vermont	6 years
Maryland	3 years	Virginia	3 years
Massachusetts	6 years	Washington	3 years
Michigan	6 years	West Virginia	5 years
Minnesota	6 years	Wisconsin	6 years
Mississippi	3 years	Wyoming	8 years
Missouri	5 years		

To figure out the amount of time you may have left on an old debt, begin counting from the date of your last payment. If there's any other payment or account—even a verbal agreement—then this may affect the start date. Check with your state's laws for details.

WRAP-UP

Getting a grip on your situation when things look bad will help you devise the correct plan for dealing with your creditors. The stronger you are, the more focused you will be to make the right decisions with your creditors.

The most important thing to remember is to take care of you and your family first. Pay only the bills that you can without jeopardizing yourself or your family. When your finances stabilize, you can resurrect your payment plans to pay off everything and make the necessary arrangements with your creditors.

COACH'S TIP

Don't allow confusion or inactivity to stop you from taking control of your financial problems. Familiarize yourself with the Fair Credit Reporting Act and the Consumer Credit Reporting Reform Act of 1996. You can obtain free copies from the Federal Trade Commission by sending a written request. Log on to www.ftc.gov for the address.

5

STARTING FROM THE BASICS

———

The best way to track and manage your money is to have a checking account and a savings account. Shop around for a bank that offers you convenience, low fees, and a level of service that suits your needs.

CHECKING ACCOUNTS

Keep an eye on the service fees. Some banks may charge you for use of their ATMs and debit cards, balance inquiries, check printing, stop payments, bounced checks, money orders, bank checks, and money market checks. Knowing which services you'll be using before signing up with a bank can help you keep these fees to a minimum. For example, there are different types of checking accounts. If you won't maintain a large balance in your account, you write a certain number of checks per month, and you occasionally use an ATM, a regular account will probably address your service needs. Banks generally charge monthly fees or charge by each check written. With the use of a regular checking account, you'll be able to write an unlimited number of checks and in most cases keep a low balance or at the very least a low minimum balance.

TYPES OF CHECKING ACCOUNTS

Here's a brief list of general accounts and their requirements:

- A regular checking account that you can get at a bank or credit union allows you to write unlimited checks, but you earn no interest on your balance. You may have to pay a per-check or monthly fee, and sometimes both. Inquire about minimum balances and possible discounts.

- An interest-bearing checking account gives you unlimited check writing ability, and you earn interest. Minimum balances are generally high. Fees can be higher than regular checking too.

- A money market deposit account offers market interest rates. If the market is doing well, you earn higher interest. Minimum balances are high, and you can expect fees if you go below the minimum. There may be some restrictions, such as limited check writing or restricted money transfers.

- A money market fund is offered through a mutual fund company. Interest is based on market conditions. Usually, no fees are charged for checks, and there is no limit on the number you can write each month. It can require a minimum balance, and there may be some restrictions on check amounts. You may not have immediate access to deposits.

- An asset management account is offered through a brokerage house or a bank that handles your investments. The primary benefit is that your banking and investment services are combined. Typically you can write unlimited checks and receive a year-end statement. It requires a high balance along with annual fees and investment fees.

BALANCING YOUR CHECKING ACCOUNT

Once you set up your account, track your money and keep your account information up to date. Some people prefer to use check ledgers, which your bank or credit union includes in your box of printed checks. Whenever you make a deposit, write checks, or withdraw money from your account, record the transaction in your ledger. By doing this you have a running total of your account balance and avoid costly overdraft fees.

When you receive your monthly bank statement, review it and compare the bank's information with your own. Note the bank's service fees in your calculations. If you cannot reconcile the two balances, these fees are frequently the culprit. You will also want to see if there are any checks you didn't write down or some ATM withdrawals you didn't enter. Perhaps an amount was transposed such as $23.40 instead of $32.40. Otherwise, you'll need to address the difference with your bank.

The easiest way to balance your checkbook is to record every purchase you make using a check, ATM or debit card.

The best method of reconciling your checkbook with your bank statement is to do the following:

1. Check off in your checkbook register each of the checks and ATM and debit cards paid by the bank. This is shown on your bank statement. This is usually in numerical sequence of the checks or the dates paid.

2. Total all outstanding checks and ATM and debit card entries that have not been paid by the bank.

3. Check off each deposit made in your check registry that has been recorded in your statement.

4. List the deposits not shown on the statement. Total the amount.

5. Write the entries in your checkbook register for any bank charges or charges using your ATM or debit card.

6. Add the ending balance on your bank statement to any deposits not shown in the statement.

7. Subtract the total outstanding checks, ATM, and debit card purchases not reported on your bank statement from the total (see #6) of your bank statement balance and deposits not reported.

8. This should give you your current balance and be equal to your checkbook balance.

SOFTWARE AND ONLINE SERVICES

Another way you can track your account is to use computer software or an online service. Both types of technology allow you to note deposits, withdrawals, and transfers. You can write checks and keep a register of them too. You'll be able to access your account balance, see which checks cleared, and determine that interest was paid, if that applies. Some systems offer personal finance tools such as a financial calendar, credit card, mortgage, and loan management, and electronic bill payment. These services make record keeping painless, and they're extremely convenient. Whichever method you select, you'll rest easier knowing exactly how much money you have at all times.

"MY HUSBAND DEALS WITH OUR CHECKING"

Maybe you're married and your spouse handles the finances. You should learn how to balance the checkbook anyway. Money issues can often create tensions in a relationship, so it's best to know what's being spent and where the money is going. If something happens to your husband, you don't want to be left out in the cold, unable to handle the checking account. Communicating and carefully handling the finances together can ease money tensions, making them a common project to be tended together versus a sparring match.

IN CASE ONE OF YOU DIES

No one likes to think of the future when it comes to anticipating a death. All too often women avoid asking the hard question, "What will I do if my husband passes away?" If your spouse is the one who deals with everything financial, you must know something about his system. And if you handle everything, let him in on the whereabouts of all the important paperwork. Create a master list detailing where everything is. Keep copies of this list in your safe deposit box and in a discreet place within your home office. Tell your spouse where this information is kept.

WHAT RECORDS SHOULD YOU LIST?

A number of important papers should be in this master file and detailed on the master list. Here's a brief list of those documents:

- Wills
- Insurance policies

- An overview of bills and their payment requirements
- Bank and creditor information
- Mortgage papers
- Investment statements
- Tax returns

Include contact names, phone numbers, addresses, and account numbers.

WILLS

If you've never dealt with this kind of paperwork before, it's a good idea to acquaint yourself with it. In case of death, the primary pertinent document is a will. A will is a legal document that, upon your death, transfers your property to beneficiaries that you've specified. In the will you appoint an executor or someone to carry out the terms of the will. If you leave behind any minor children, then you should specify a guardian as well. In order for the will to be considered authentic, it needs to have your signature and the signatures of two witnesses who watched you sign the document.

You can change the terms of your will by creating a completely new one or by using a codicil. A codicil is a legal term for a written amendment that affects and alters certain clauses within the initial will. To make things easier, have copies only of current wills on hand. Retaining older copies will confuse the process in the event that you or your spouse dies. You are wise to consult an attorney to properly prepare your will. There are do-it-yourself will-kits available, but in all cases it's a good idea to have an attorney review what you have done.

INTESTATE

What happens if there is no will? This is called "Intestate." Basically the state where you reside administers your estate, and settlement is handled through a probate court—often a time-consuming and expensive process. Also, depending upon the laws in your state, there may be some surprises as to how the estate is handled. For example, in some states, if you remarried but have children only from the first marriage, your spouse could receive all of your estate and your children nothing at all. To control the settlement of your estates, you and your husband must have wills.

A LIVING WILL

You may have heard the term "living will." A living will expresses your wishes about whether you want to be kept alive should you become terminally ill or seriously injured.

WHAT IS AN ESTATE?

Your estate is comprised of assets. Assets can be anything that you own, such as bank accounts, investment accounts, retirement accounts, real estate, and life insurance policies. Your assets must have your name on them.

If you're married, half of everything that you jointly own with your spouse is considered to be part of your estate. If you are a partner in or a sole owner of a business, this is also part of your estate. If you're a trustee or custodian of property that you've put in a revocable trust (a trust you can modify once it has been set up), or a custodial account (a gift account for a minor that doesn't incur the gift tax), this is considered part of your estate. And finally any outstanding money that may be owed to you is part of your estate.

Certain liabilities will reduce your estate. They include taxes owed, outstanding debt, and estate settlement costs.

Upon someone's death, the value of the estate in question is calculated by determining the federal estate and state inheritance taxes. Your heirs will owe these amounts unless you've made provisions for them in your will. Contact an attorney to make sure these papers are handled properly.

MORTGAGES

If you own real estate and there is a balance owed, you will need to have a copy of the note and deed of trust. The note outlines the agreement between you and the lender regarding the property you own and the mortgage amount. When you purchased your home or property, you received important documents such as: truth in lending statements, escrow papers, title reports, title insurance, proof of insurance, loan notes, certificates of occupancy, and closing statements.

These documents are associated with the purchase of your home. They should be kept together, along with any refinancing, home equity, or home insurance papers, as well as copies of quit-claim deeds (if a property was deeded in your name) or a copy of a reconveyence from a lender who has been paid off with your loan.

TAX RECORDS

Tax records must generally be kept at least three years and, if you have the room, seven. The three-year date correlates to a time frame, called a period of limitations, that the IRS usually has to audit income tax paperwork that you've filed from a given year. There are certain circumstances that may require you to keep records beyond three years. By visiting www.irs.gov, you can obtain a copy of Publication 552: *Record-keeping for Individuals*. It should answer any questions.

Records that you should hold onto include but are not limited to:

- Copies of employee check stubs

- Income sources that pay interest

- Companies that pay you dividends

- Anything that relates to or provides information about your earnings

- W-2 forms

- 1099 forms

If you're retired, keep your 1099R forms because they detail the sources of your retirement income.

Any time the IRS or state requests an audit, you'll need to have copies or evidence of expenses that you claimed in your tax return. These would include receipts and canceled checks, which are standard forms of evidence. These are also considered valid: credit charge slips (note the expense reasons on the back) and an appointment book or expense ledger with details, costs, meeting notes, and purchases.

Some things require special records. For instance, if you or your spouse receives tips, there's a specific way to handle them. Likewise, non-cash charitable donations need to be dealt with in a particular manner. The IRS publishes materials that address these needs. You can request information from www.irs.gov or consult your accountant or person who prepares your tax return.

INVESTMENTS

In regard to investment paperwork, account statements will give you details on your financial position. Brokerage records will list security trades made during an account period. A summary of income lists each security owned, plus dividends, capital gains, and interest, so you'll want to have these on hand. Mutual funds issue regular statements outlining deposits, withdrawals, capital gains, and distributions.

Mutual funds also have year-end summaries, so keep them with the statements. Confirmation statements give information on any buy/sell activity, specifically the transaction type, where the exchange was made, and the terms and conditions. A brokerage summary will provide information on all your investments, detailing the market value of all your stocks, bonds, and mutual funds. IRA information may be on a separate report.

LIFE INSURANCE POLICIES

You'll want to familiarize yourself with any life insurance policies taken out on you or your spouse. In case of the death or disability of an income provider, life insurance is intended to cover a dependent's or family's financial needs. Here are things you'll want to know about a policy:

- The type of coverage
- The company name
- How long payments have been made
- Agent's name and telephone number

WRAP-UP

It may be hard to think about some of these things, and they may seem somewhat overwhelming. However, you must understand what kinds of paperwork are critical to your lifestyle and where they are located. Part of financial security is thinking about the future and planning for an emergency or sudden death of a loved one. It's best to be safe and knowledgeable rather than sorry. When such events happen, sudden demands are forced upon us. The more you know about handling your finances, the easier it will be on you to get control and eliminate the stress. It will be easier on you and your family if important paperwork is organized and ready for settlement.

COACH'S TIP

Setting up an organized system for your financial records can eliminate frustration and keep you on top of your bills and taxes. Don't make the mistake of keeping sloppy files, because that will only undermine your financial efforts.

Do allot a set time for paying bills and balancing your checkbook. You'll feel more in control when you practice good money management.

6

THE REPORT THAT SAYS IT ALL

Have you ever seen a copy of your credit report? A credit report is essentially a summary document that tracks how you use your credit. Three credit reporting agencies collect this information within the United States: Equifax, Experian, and Trans Union.

These credit reporting agencies are huge databases that continuously record information on anyone who has credit.

Since consumers are constantly using their credit, the information on these reports is always being updated. Due to the sheer volume of data, credit reporting is a big business, and each credit reporting agency is in direct competition with the other. The reporting agencies make their money by providing the credit information they gather to fee-paying subscribers who are credit grantors, such as banks, insurers, retailers, potential employers, and others.

AUTHORIZED USAGE

There are guidelines about who can access this information. Whenever you apply for a line of credit, you will see a signature line that asks for your permission to have your report reviewed by a potential credit grantor. Your signature indicates your agreement to have this information provided to the creditor listed on the application. If you view your credit report and see an inquiry that you have not authorized, you need to make note of it and contact the party involved immediately! Your credit report contains highly personal and discretionary information, so you want to ensure that it's well protected.

Excessive inquiries within a six-month period are looked upon unfavorably by potential creditors and may result in a credit denial. If you have unauthorized inquiries, contact the party, and ask that this information be removed from your record.

Never give out information such as your name, address, Social Security number, and birth date to anyone, especially by phone, unless you know the purpose for the request and feel the request is legitimate. Identity theft has become a serious—and costly—problem.

WHERE YOUR CREDIT HISTORY COMES FROM

Creditors provide credit report information. After you've been granted credit, permission to report your charge and payment habits is included in the creditor's standard terms and disclosures, which you agree to when you accept the credit. From there you are constantly being observed for where you shop, how much debt you incur, how much of your overall debt you pay off, whether you pay on time, what types of credit you use, and so on. That's why it's important to pay your bills on time and to communicate with your lenders when there's a problem because all of this information will affect you at some point.

Let's say you want to buy a car. Unless you have cash to pay for everything, you'll need to take out a loan of some kind. When you do so, a dealership will run a credit check on you. If your report shows that you are unreliable, you will be considered a credit risk. Your chances of being approved will consequently be very slim.

Anytime you are granted a line of credit, you're being trusted to pay back any debts you incur. It is not a responsibility to be treated lightly.

In addition to creditors, the reporting agencies will use other sources to gather information on your credit habits. Public records such as tax liens, bankruptcies, judgments, and other public notices are closely watched. For instance, if you become overwhelmed by debt and decide to file for bankruptcy, the credit reporting agencies will report the filing on your credit report.

WHAT INFORMATION IS ON MY REPORT?

Information that appears on your credit report includes your name, your address, your previous addresses, your Social Security number, your birth date, your employer's name and address, and current and previous creditor accounts. There will also be specific details on the type of credit: for example, who is the primary person responsible for the account, the terms of the credit, account limits, account activity, most recent balances, and a general comments area. Creditors are the ones who actually evaluate your credit usage, not the credit reporting agencies.

Not all creditors subscribe to all three credit reporting agencies. You may wonder how this affects you. Say you apply for credit from Friendly Loans, and they subscribe only to Experian. Then that's where they'll receive their credit check information. If you have a negative item reported on your Equifax report, Friendly Loans may not see it because they subscribe only to Experian. If you want to determine what is being reported about your credit history, you'll need to request copies of your credit report from all three agencies.

Negative or positive information can stay on your credit report only a specific period of time. Some states may differ, but the majority of states indicate that charge-offs, slow payments, delinquent payments, collection accounts, judgments, paid tax liens, and repossessions can remain on your credit report up to seven years from the date of the last activity on the account.

A bankruptcy can remain on your credit report up to ten years from the filing date.

All inquiries can remain on your credit report up to two years from the date of the inquiry.

After the period of time elapses, these items should be automatically removed.

REQUESTING YOUR CREDIT REPORT

To obtain copies of your credit report, you can write a letter to each agency or order your credit report at the credit reporting agencies' Web sites. If you write to the agency to order your credit report, include a check or money order to cover the report fees, which average $8 per report. If you are also requesting your FICO score with your report, some agencies charge a higher fee. I recommend you request your FICO score to see what areas you need to improve. If you order your credit report online, you will need a credit card to pay the fee. Every state has a different fee, so call, write, or visit the credit reporting agencies' Web sites to get the correct fees for your state. You'll need to provide your name, address, Social Security number, and a copy of your driver's license or a recent bill (a utility bill or a credit card bill) to verify your identification.

Some states allow one or two complimentary credit reports per year. Contact the credit reporting agency before ordering to see whether your state requires a fee.

To request a copy of your credit report, write, call, or visit the credit reporting agencies' Web sites: Equifax, P.O. Box 105873, Atlanta, GA 30348, 800-685-1111, www.equifax.com;

Experian, P.O. Box 2104, Allen, TX 75013-2104, 888-397-3742, www.experian.com; and Trans Union, P.O. Box 1000, Chester, PA 19022, 800-888-4213, www.tuc.com.

IF YOU'VE APPLIED FOR CREDIT BUT BEEN TURNED DOWN

If you've recently applied for credit but been turned down, you can request a free copy from the reporting agency used. Your request must be received within sixty days of your receipt of the credit denial letter. The denial letter will list the name of the reporting agency and the appropriate address. When making your request, mention the name of the company that denied your application, and include your name, address, and Social Security number.

You can receive a free report only from the agency listed on the denial letter. You will not be able to receive free reports from all three agencies using that one particular letter. If the company isn't listed as an inquiry, you must pay for the report. Also, if you're married, you must apply individually even though you may have joint accounts.

UNDERSTANDING AND EVALUATING YOUR REPORT

When you receive copies of all three reports, sit down and review them. Each reporting agency has its own format, which means you'll have to decipher each report individually. They all try to present their information in a user-friendly way, and you'll find an explanation section on the report itself.

As you begin your review, check each item listed on the report for the correct name, address, and Social Security number. With the amount of information that these agencies handle, there's a good chance that you'll find inaccuracies and errors on your report. The average rate is approximately 70 percent—another reason why you should review your report on a consistent basis.

Next, determine the status of each account. If you're looking at an Equifax report, find the column labeled "CS." All ratings are listed here. Equifax uses ratings such as I-3, R-1, and R-7. These ratings have a coded meaning. An I-3 says that you were three months late paying your account, an R-1 is a positive rating and tells a creditor that you pay within your thirty-day billing cycle or the agreed time frame of the account, and an R-7 indicates that you're making regular payments on a wage-earner plan or other such arrangement. There are a number of codes, so refer to Equifax's explanation for full details; however, anything other than an R-1 or I-1 rating is considered negative. The "R" stands for a revolving account, and the "I" means an installment account. The numbers refer to the actual rating with one essentially translating to an account that is current. Scrutinize each item for accuracy. If it shows that you made a late payment and you didn't, you can and should dispute this information.

On an Experian report, look at the listed items. They are numbered, and if a dash appears on both sides of the number next to an item, this is a negative or derogatory entry. It will look something like this: Item -1- Big Business Company shows your account as thirty days late. If you see these dashes, read the entire entry. It should tell you whether this entry is a late payment, a charge-off, an account that went to collection, or a public notice such as a bankruptcy, tax lien, or judgment. Again, really analyze what's being reported. Even if you made a late payment but your report shows an even later payment, you can dispute that because it's inaccurate.

Trans Union's reports actually separate the negative information from the positive. Negative and derogatory information is contained within brackets (> <), placed on the upper portion of the report. Your positive or nonadverse information is on the lower portion of the report. Again, review each entry for accuracy.

REPAIRING YOUR CREDIT REPORT

Dispute any incomplete, incorrect, inaccurate, or erroneous information on your report. You must handle disputes separately with each agency. Just because one reporting agency removes an inaccuracy from its report doesn't mean that the information comes off the other two.

For each report entry, ensure that it is your account, the account numbers are correct, the dates and the amounts are right, the dates of the last activity are correct, and the rating is accurate. Incorrect information will require a dispute letter detailing the problem. Your letter should also indicate your name, address, and Social Security number. Never put more than four items you're disputing in one letter. For example, if eight inaccurate items appeared on your credit report, you would write two letters including only four items of dispute per each letter. It's best to have a thirty-day interim between multiple dispute letters. The reason behind splitting disputed items is that, in the long run, it's easier for you to track their investigations and make sure they're properly conducted. Expect to receive an updated report from the credit reporting agency within forty-five days of the agency's receipt of your letter. If the disputed items cannot be verified or if the creditor doesn't respond, the item will be removed from your report.

If the creditor does respond and indicates that the item is correct, then the entry will remain on your report. The agency has thirty days to finalize its investigation from the receipt of your dispute letter. If you're still unsatisfied with the outcome, you can submit a one hundred-word statement, explaining your version of the disputed item, and have it added to your report. You can do this for each disputed entry.

In a situation where you have evidence or documentation showing that a disputed entry is incorrect, you can attach a copy to your dispute letter to the credit reporting agency. For example, you might have a letter or statement proving that you paid an account that is still showing a balance. If this is the case, mail it in with your dispute letter. Doing this will expedite your dispute by making it easier for the reporting agency to conduct its investigation.

Another way to correct your report is to directly approach the creditor. Write a letter informing the firm that it is providing incorrect or inaccurate information on your account. Request a letter detailing the correction and have it sent to the credit reporting agencies too. When you receive this letter from the creditor, make a copy and then attach it to your dispute letter. Send your letter and the attachment to the credit reporting agencies to be absolutely sure that the dispute has been duly noted and corrected.

To assist you in this process, I've provided sample dispute letters: Remember to dispute all three credit reporting agencies if necessary. Also, look at the dates.

SAMPLE LETTER 1

Date 6/20/01
Dear Trans Union,

A recent review of my credit report reveals the following errors:
Big Business Co., account 00000101 is not my account.
Friendly Loan, account 777777777 was not paid thirty days late. Refer to the attached billing statement.

Easy Credit Inc., account 555555555 was paid in full as of August 2000. There is no outstanding balance on this account.

Kindly look into each of these disputed entries. When you've finished your investigation, update my credit report accordingly.

SAMPLE LETTER 2

Date 7/20/01
Dear Trans Union,

A recent review of my credit report reveals the following errors:

Your Local Business, Inc., account 00000062656 is not my account. My middle initial is A. and not M.

Big Money Loan, account 7256400007 was not paid late, refer to the attached billing statement for the proper payment date.

E-Z-2 Get Credit Inc., account 19191919191917 has been closed. The account balance was transferred to another card as of June 2001.

Kindly look into each of these disputed entries. When you've finished your investigation, update my credit report accordingly.

THE FAIR CREDIT REPORTING ACT

The Federal Trade Commission regulates credit reporting agencies. Under provisions outlined in the Fair Credit Reporting Act and the Consumer Credit Reporting Reform Act of 1996, you have the right to dispute any items on your report that you feel are incomplete, incorrect, inaccurate, or erroneous.

Upon receiving your dispute letter, the reporting agency has thirty days to complete its investigation. Disputed information must be removed if it proves to be inaccurate or unverifiable, or if the creditor doesn't respond.

If the creditor reasserts that its information is correct, the item will stay on the report, but you can write a one hundred-word statement on the item of dispute, explaining the issue and why you feel it's inaccurate. This statement will appear on your report for potential creditors to see. If you don't want to write a statement, then upon receipt of your updated credit report, wait another 120 days from the date of the last updated credit report and try disputing the remaining items again.

Keep repeating this procedure. The reporting agency must continue investigating the matter unless it finds it frivolous or irrelevant.

FICO SCORES

Until quite recently your FICO score was top secret. A FICO score is commonly used throughout the lending industry to quickly identify whether a potential applicant is creditworthy. When you apply for a credit card, a mortgage, or a bank loan, the creditor will check your credit report and your FICO score. The initials are derived from the scoring system developed by Fair, Isaac and Co.

There are other credit bureau scores besides the FICO score, and some lenders may incorporate a FICO score into their own system. If you're working with a lender that subscribes to Equifax, the FICO score can also be referred to as a BEACON score. Experian uses the Experian/Fair, Isaac Risk Model, and Trans Union has the EMPIRICA score. Essentially Fair, Isaac and Co. has developed all of these scores so that explains why FICO is the most common term used throughout the lending industry.

HOW IS YOUR FICO SCORE CALCULATED?

Your FICO score is calculated using several variables that include but are not limited to these:

- Total amount of credit you already have

- Number of credit inquiries within the past year

- Payment history

- Amounts owed

- Length of credit history

- Types of credit used

This information is averaged into a three-digit number. These scores can range from 300 to 900. Most lenders prefer to see a score of 700 or above for credit approval but scores above 620 will still get you good rates.

Before submitting an application, find out your FICO score. You can go online to www.myfico.com to get the score directly from Fair, Isaac. You can also visit www.Qspace.com, which offers the same service for a small fee. E-LOAN (*www.eloan.com*) has been offering free credit scores online for some time and has been a factor in making these scores available to the general public.

LOW FICO SCORE?

If your FICO score is low, you may want to contact a credit rescorer. This relatively new business service is being offered by local credit reporting agencies nationwide. Check local listings to see whether such a service is available in your area, or ask your lender to refer you to a reliable rescoring expert. The three large credit bureaus—Equifax, Experian, and Tran Union—are not affiliated with this service. The service allows lenders to request that an applicant's credit files be rescored at each of the three large credit reporting agencies.

How does this work? A rescorer goes through your files, carefully reviewing any negative entries you may have. Sometimes, these "derogatories" are inaccuracies or errors. The rescorer obtains written corrections of these entries and then sends them to the three credit reporting agencies.

A rescorer also evaluates your current debt, then advises you on how to restructure certain information—information that may have caused a creditor to reject your loan application. For example, you may have high outstanding balances on your credit cards. But you don't want high credit card balances when your FICO score is pulled. The rescorer will explain ways to redistribute or pay off these balances so that your application will be approved. Such advice can result in a raised FICO score.

WRAP-UP

Knowing what's on your credit report and how to improve your credit report and FICO score is a financial fundamental. Whether you're single or married, you need to obtain a copy of your report on a six-month to yearly basis. Think of the large percentage of errors that are reported if you need motivation to do this. After all, your credit report represents your credit worthiness. Whenever you wish to purchase a big-ticket item, take out a cash advance, apply for a home loan, or rent an apartment, a credit check will be run, and you'll be judged by what appears on your report.

If you want to attain financial security, ensure that your report accurately presents your credit history by consistently and systematically reviewing it. If you've had problems in the past, working with your report will help you stay focused on changing your habits. You'll ultimately gain a new sense of confidence in knowing that you are a duly responsible and conscientious consumer, a good credit risk.

COACH'S TIP

Don't try to clean up your credit while you're in the process of making a large purchase or trying to qualify for a loan. You don't want a potential creditor to see sudden drastic changes, such as decreasing the number of cards you have from seven to two. Instead, plan ahead and see that everything is in place before you approach potential creditors.

7

WILL YOU MAKE IT?
QUALIFYING AND APPLYING FOR CREDIT

Every woman should have credit of her own. With so many women in the workforce, it's even more critical that women obtain and manage their own credit. If you are married and don't have a joint account with your spouse, or you are listed as a user on someone else's card, you really don't have credit that's your very own. This may not affect you right now. However, should anything happen to your husband or the primary holder of the card, establishing credit on your own will be extremely difficult, especially if time is an issue for you. If you're single and have no credit, you have nothing to fall back on in an emergency. Granted, no one likes to think of such things, but now that you're taking charge of your financial security, you need to honestly assess your situation and plan ahead.

ESTABLISHING CREDIT

What do creditors look for? Basically they want to make sure that you can repay any debts you incur and that you do so in a responsible and timely manner. In other words, creditors want you to have the three C's of credit:

1. Capacity
2. Character
3. Collateral

1. CAPACITY

Let's consider capacity first. When you fill out a credit application, you'll be asked questions about employment, such as what your present position is, who employs you, and how long you've been employed in this position. Creditors will consider how long you've been in a particular line of work, and whether you're self-employed or paid on a commission-only basis. Creditors will inquire about your yearly income, including bonuses or outside money sources.

Next, they'll want to know about your expenses. Do you have any dependents? Do you pay child support or alimony? They want to determine the total amount of your outgoing costs. They'll consider the amount of the item or loan you're requesting credit for too. If you're applying for a credit card, mortgage, or car loan, the creditor will calculate the amount of credit you can afford in light of your expenses.

DEBT TO INCOME RATIO

How do creditors figure out your capacity for debt? They use a standard formula called a debt to income ratio. They start out by calculating your total monthly debt or expenses, which include your rent or mortgage payments, car payments, insurance, credit card payments, alimony, child support, and so on. When figuring this number, creditors include the monthly payment of the item that you want to finance. Next, they'll divide this number by your total monthly gross (before taxes) income. If the debt ratio is more than 50 percent, most likely you will be denied credit.

WORKOUT

Calculating Your Debt to Income Ratio

Gross Monthly Income		Monthly Fixed Income	
Salary	$_____	Rent or mortgage	$_____
Spouse salary	_____	Automobile	_____
Commissions	_____	Automobile	_____
Bonuses	_____	Bank installments	_____
Alimony	_____	Charge/revolving accts.	_____
Child support	_____	Child support	_____
Other	_____	Alimony	_____
		Other	_____
Total income	$_____	Other	_____
(Before taxes)		Proposed loan payment	_____
		Total payments	$_____

The total monthly payments divided by the total monthly gross income equals your debt ratio. If the ratio is more than 50 percent, the banks may not approve the loan. Before you apply for credit, speak with the lending institution about its loan to debt ratio policies.

PRECAUTIONARY STEPS

Because you want to avoid excessive inquiries on your credit report, it's a good idea to take a few precautionary steps before you apply.

Contact the creditor to find out what it accepts as an approved debt to income ratio. Then calculate your debt to income ratio using the formula: monthly debt divided by monthly income. If your ratio is higher than the accepted rate or is just too high in and of itself (above 50 percent), do not submit an application.

2. CHARACTER

Here's where responsible handling of your finances pays off. Creditors will contact a credit reporting agency to determine your credit history and your payment patterns. They'll run a credit check on you using Equifax, Experian, or Trans Union. Generally they check with one agency, but it's possible that they'll contact all three agencies. If your FICO score is too low, you will be denied the credit.

Ideally they're looking for stable, reliable income earners—even taking into account whether you own or rent your home and how long you've been at that residence. Creditors prefer to approve lines of credit for individuals who have resided in one place at least two years; long-term residency definitely enhances the chances of approval. If you move around frequently, creditors may not feel comfortable granting you credit.

Creditors are primarily interested in a solid payment history, because it makes them feel more comfortable in granting you credit. If you've had some negative payment patterns in your past, you should have at least two or three accounts that show a good payment history established since your problems. Having no credit at all is considered the same as having negative or bad credit. This is another reason why every woman seeking financial security should obtain credit of her own.

3. COLLATERAL

Assets, or collateral, are another aspect of your financial background of interest to creditors. They view assets as a possible way to recoup their money should you stop making payments on a loan or debt. Assets include savings accounts, investments, and property.

Being strong in one aspect of the three C's will not guarantee credit approval. Creditors review all three elements—capacity, character, and collateral—when considering your credit application. You greatly improve your chances for approval when each area is sound.

PREPARING TO APPLY FOR CREDIT

You should know a number of things before submitting a credit application. With a little bit of homework, you may avoid being denied credit as well as having unnecessary credit. Doing some preparatory work will also pay off in the long run because you won't have excessive inquiries or records of being denied credit on your report.

The first thing to do is to request copies of all your reports from the three credit reporting agencies: Equifax, Experian, and Trans Union.

Upon receiving your reports, review each one thoroughly. Double-check everything: your name, address, Social Security number, account numbers, payment information, and account status. If you find any errors, correct them before making an application.

Once you know what's on your reports, contact the creditor and ask which credit reporting agency it uses. Since you already have copies from each agency, you'll immediately know what information the creditor will see when reviewing your records. But if the creditor indicates that it uses a credit report that reflects negative or derogatory information about your credit history, avoid applying for that credit. For example, if your Experian report looks good, and that's what the creditor uses, then go ahead and apply. However, if the creditor uses Trans Union and that report has problems on it, do not apply.

PROTECTING YOUR CREDIT INFORMATION

Be discreet when giving out information related to your credit history. Never give your name, address, or Social Security number to anyone over the phone, unless you are explicitly authorizing them to run a credit check on you. In this instance, make sure that you're dealing with a reputable business or company prior to providing that information. Although this may appear overly cautious to you, you should be aware that you run the risk of someone stealing your private information, which could potentially result in someone using your identity to open up credit. There's also the matter of excessive inquiries showing up on your credit report.

MY STORY
Several years ago my husband, Hal, and I were looking for a new car. Hal was on the telephone talking to an automobile broker. I heard him giving the broker his Social Security number, address, and birth date.

I rushed into the kitchen where he was talking and started waving my arms to stop him from giving this information. Hal's signal to me was not to worry, he had everything under control.

When he hung up from his call, he told me the broker needed the information for his files. Of course, I thought differently and decided to follow up.

Several weeks later, we decided against buying a new car. I requested copies of our credit reports from the credit reporting agencies and discovered six unauthorized inquiries. Each inquiry was from the broker shopping for a loan. He had misrepresented himself to Hal.

I quickly telephoned the broker and asked where he got the authorization to run our credit reports. He began to stutter and stammer because he had been caught.

I reminded him of the Fair Credit Reporting Act and indicated that he must have these inquiries removed since they were never authorized. I gave him two weeks to do it and indicated I would pursue the issue further if they were not removed.

At the end of two weeks, I ordered another copy of the credit reports, and all the inquiries were removed. If I had not known my legal rights, our credit reports would have been damaged.

IDENTITY THEFT

Another reason to guard your personal information carefully is identity theft: a thief obtains your information and then uses it to make unauthorized charges. In the U.S. alone, 400,000 people will have had their identity stolen. And they usually found out about it through a charge that is denied approval or a creditor call.

Undoing the thief's work is time consuming. Depending upon the situation, estimate eight months and even up to a couple of years to clean up your credit records.

Here are steps to take when your identity has been stolen:

- Contact each of the three credit reporting agencies and request that a fraud alert notice be placed on your report.

- Ask that creditors contact you before opening any accounts using your name.

- Check with your credit card companies to see if your account has had any changes or unauthorized charges. Write them about your situation.

- File a police report. Send copies to the credit reporting agencies and your creditors.

- Contact the Office of the Inspector General at the fraud hot line (800) 786-2551, or visit the Web site www.nara.gov.

STANDARD QUESTIONS TO ASK
A POTENTIAL CREDITOR

Before submitting an application, ask the creditor some standard questions regarding terms, such as: What is the yearly or annual rate?

A number of credit card companies charge a yearly fee to use their cards. These fees can range from $18 to $40. Other credit card companies don't charge an annual fee.

Some credit card companies divide their annual fees into twelve months and charge you monthly. For example, if your annual fee is $36, the bank charges you $3 per month toward your annual fee. This is an annoyance, especially if you aren't using the card. To avoid this, prepay the annual fee. It will reflect as a credit on your credit card statement, but that is better than having to pay a proportional fee.

INTEREST RATES

What is your interest rate, and how is it calculated?

There are two standard ways to figure interest rates. Some companies begin charging interest from the date an item is purchased. Others charge interest on a prorated basis; between the time of the purchase and the time your bill is due, you're extended a grace or "float" period where no interest is being charged. Instead, they'll calculate interest from the time the bill is due and onward. Consequently if you make a purchase at the beginning of your billing cycle, you have the remaining days to use the credit company's money interest free.

If you take advantage of these grace periods, pay off the balance when the bill is due. Otherwise, you will pay interest, which defeats the point of using the institution's money without having to pay interest. You want to get into the habit of paying off your credit cards in full each month. Not doing so puts you in a position where you can accumulate bad debt or overextend yourself. By paying only the minimum monthly payment, interest will continue to accrue, which is adding to the principal amount, and your balance will increase.

TYPES OF CARDS AND CREDIT LIMITS

The next question you should ask the creditor is: What cards do you issue, and what are their credit limits?

Some companies offer one type of card while others offer more than one. Knowing which ones are available will help you determine which one is right for you.

I recommend having two or three credit cards with low interest rates. It's easier to prudently track and manage two or three cards than it is to have many cards with high interest rates. For most of us, having too many cards is just too tempting and can quickly result in becoming overextended and in debt. Credit cards should be used primarily to take care of an emergency and to establish a payment history on your credit report.

NEWLY ESTABLISHED CREDIT

If you're just starting to establish your credit, you'll want to know how often the company considers your account for credit increases.

Most companies generally look at your account history once every six months. Some companies review your account only once a year. If you want to build up your credit history, apply to a company that has a six-month review. Then pay off your monthly balance, or at the very least, pay more than the minimum balance. Stay below your credit limit. If you let your balance go over this limit, you'll be denied an increase when it is time for your account review.

Most companies charge a fee or have a higher interest rate on cash advances. To make sure you understand the company's terms, ask, What charges will be assessed if I take out a cash advance? What is the maximum amount I can take out?

It's typical for you to be advanced 100 percent of your credit limit. However, if you're carrying a balance, you'll be able to take out an amount based on your available credit. If you've been given courtesy checks with your account, you'll be charged the same fees for using them as you would for taking out a cash advance.

COMPLETING YOUR CREDIT APPLICATION

Whenever you fill out a credit application, thoroughly review everything, and complete all the information fields. Creditors may choose to verify all the information that you've given them, so be truthful about any details. Don't exaggerate any information.

BASIC INFORMATION

Give your full name, including your middle name or initial. Provide your present address, along with your previous one. Next, supply the name of your employer, your current position, and your income. Be honest about your income because creditors may contact your employer to verify this amount. If your employer quotes a lesser amount, your credit application will be denied.

You'll be asked to provide credit information or liabilities. Use the information listed on your credit reports to fill out this section, especially the amount of your outstanding debt. Since the creditors will be looking at the same reports, there should be no discrepancies.

For your mortgage and/or rental information, include the name, address, telephone number, account number, payment, and balances of your mortgage company or landlord.

If the creditor wants your tax return, attach a copy of your W-2 or 1099 form to your application. Don't send the original, which should remain part of your financial records. A creditor may use your tax forms to verify your income.

FINANCIAL RECORDS

Establishing and maintaining a good records system will eliminate stress from your life because it's never pleasant to search through piles of papers to find forms or bills. If that's how your paperwork is currently "filed," you'll only end up frustrated when you deal with your finances.

Take the time to set up your files. Once your system is in place, you'll have access to accurate information, whether you're filling out a credit application or completing your tax return.

Proper maintenance of your finances lets you see exactly where you spend your money and how much debt you've incurred. You can also track your savings and assets. Ultimately you'll discover that being familiar with all this information can assist you in setting financial goals, both short and long term, and achieving them.

READ THE DISCLOSURES!

Most of us are familiar with the old adage, "read the fine print." When you deal with credit, that's especially true. Although credit can be a wonderful tool if used properly, too many of us forget that it's a business. By not reading the fine print, we take on responsibility without genuinely understanding what we've agreed to, which can lead to trouble.

And when you receive your credit card, read the inserts that come with your billing statement. Many times the inserts are a change of terms on your contract. Don't be the last one to find out your interest rate increased.

Under the Truth in Lending Act, all creditors and lenders are required to list their disclosures. Usually you'll find them printed on the back of the application or on a separate insert. Prior to doing anything else, read these disclosures! Knowing the standard terms helps you determine whether this line of credit is appropriate for you.

Reading the disclosures isn't enough, however. Specifically look for the following:

- APR (annual percentage rate)

- Finance charges

- Interest rates

- Cash advances (fees or higher interest rates?)

- Computation of credit balances

- Calculation of interest rates

- Grace period

- Annual fees

- Over-the-limit charges

- Overdraft fees

- Late fees

Carefully consider all of these items, and shop for the best deal available. After all, you want your credit to work for you.

AUTHORIZATION

Now that you've read the fine print, you've determined that you want to make an application. But there's one more thing you must review. At the bottom of the form, underneath the signature line, is more fine print. This is the authorization statement. By signing here, you give creditors permission to verify all the information that you've just provided. They can check your bank account information, your employment situation, and any other references that you've given them.

Additionally, you've authorized them to obtain a copy of your credit report and consult with any of your creditors about you. If they grant you credit, this statement allows the creditors to report your credit history to the reporting agencies. You're also stating that all information contained within the application is accurate and that you understand and agree to all the terms and agreements (disclosures) of this credit application.

WRAP-UP

Applying for credit is a lot of work. Knowing how the process works is the key to successfully obtaining the credit you want. If you practice solid financial habits and keep your focus on your short-and-long term goals, you should be well on your way to attaining financial security.

Again, I cannot stress how important it is for women to have their own credit and to carefully manage it. Having credit is a big responsibility. In today's world you'll often be asked if you have a credit card to secure a reservation for a hotel, to rent a car, to purchase airline tickets, or make internet purchases. Credit is basically a way of life for our society. Avail yourself of credit, and above all, establish and maintain a good credit history.

COACH'S TIP

Avoid identity theft! Should someone use your name and information to make charges, it will take both time and money to clean up your credit report. Heed these cautions:

- Do not carry your Social Security card in your wallet along with your other major forms of identification, such as your drivers license. If your wallet or purse is stolen, the thief won't have access to all of your information.

- Be careful with your mail. Don't leave your bills or solicitations out where someone could steal them and obtain your information. Use locked mailboxes or drop your bills off at the post office.

- Thieves go through dumpsters or garbage cans to come up with credit slips, bill statements, and other finance-related documents. Shred all your documents before throwing them out.

8

You Have to Start Somewhere

———

You've decided that you want to establish credit of your own. If you don't have credit, it's hard to get credit. As a matter of fact, having no credit history is just as bad as having negative credit. The reason is that the creditors have no way of reviewing your payment history on a credit report. Nonetheless, there are ways to establish it. We're going to discuss several approaches you can take to open that first line of credit.

FIRST-TIME CREDIT

When you are approved for credit, you need to remember your financial goals. The primary purpose of opening up your first lines of credit is to establish your credit history.

If you are getting credit so that you can purchase things you typically couldn't afford, then you're putting yourself in a potentially precarious financial position. It's the job of marketers and retailers to entice you into making a purchase today and then paying for it over an extended period of time. Don't fall into that trap! You'll end up paying more for the item than its original price, and you may wind up overextended on your credit to boot.

Develop and maintain sound credit habits from the start. You work hard for your money, so use it and save it responsibly.

WOMEN AND CREDIT

I've already mentioned how important I think it is for women to have credit of their own. To better understand this point, read these stories about other women.

JULIE'S STORY

Julie had been married for several years. She handled the finances in her home, but all the credit was under her husband's name. Julie was a capable financial manager, paying everything in a timely manner. But when she decided to apply for a credit card in her own name, Julie was turned down. This surprised her. Her application was denied because there was no credit record under her name. Everything was reported in her husband's name and not hers.

DINA'S STORY

Recently divorced, Dina was busy trying to reestablish her life. She decided to reassume her maiden name. Now that she no longer shared joint finances with her ex-husband, she decided to apply for her own credit. When she was turned down, Dina was taken aback. She'd previously had good standing with her open accounts, but they were all under her married name. Consequently no record existed of her credit history when she used her maiden name.

MARGARET'S STORY

Margaret was in her mid-twenties. She was single, and up to this point in her life, she had paid cash for everything. When she considered applying for credit, she didn't have a clue about how she should proceed. Of course, because she'd never had credit, she was finding it difficult to establish it. How could she build a solid credit record when no one was willing to approve her application?

KATHLEEN'S STORY

Kathleen had been married for four years and had established two lines of credit in her name separate from her husband.

During the fifth year of their marriage, Kathleen's husband was laid off from his job. They fell behind on paying their bills. Kathleen was able to hang on to her two credit cards and continued to make minimum payments.

Once Kathleen's husband began working again, their credit report was bad. Kathleen's credit cards were the only cards that still were in good standing.

When things settled down, Kathleen was able to add her husband's name onto her credit cards, helping him to reestablish good credit on his credit report.

All four of these scenarios are common. That's why I stress the importance of planning ahead and securing your own credit line, especially if you're a woman. You can avoid all of these situations with a little forethought and even help your husband rebuild his credit.

BASIC CREDIT GUIDELINES

The following guidelines will help women who are facing some of the issues presented in these stories.

If you've had credit before, but it was under your maiden name, contact your creditors and the credit reporting agencies to inform them of your married name, along with any other pertinent information that may have changed. Instruct them to update their files and your credit report. It's a good idea to request your report from all three credit reporting agencies several weeks later to ensure your requests have been processed and recorded.

If you had a joint account with your husband or former husband, and aren't sure whether your payment patterns have been reported on your credit report, request copies of your credit report from all three credit reporting agencies. Review each credit report to see if the accounts in question are duly noted. If not, contact the creditors, and request that they update their records. Be sure to have them update your credit report. After a few weeks, reorder your report to ensure that the changes have been implemented.

Since credit reports are under individual names, it's a good idea to let each creditor know that even though you are married, you want joint account information reported on your and your husband's reports.

If you were recently divorced and have changed your name, contact your creditors, and inform them of this change. Have them update your accounts and notify the credit reporting agency of these changes.

SECURED CREDIT CARDS

A secured credit card allows you to open an account by depositing a sum of money with a bank, credit union, or savings and loan. The bank or creditor issues you a Visa or MasterCard that is secured by this deposit. For example, the creditor may require you to deposit $350 into the account; the $350 would be your credit limit.

A secured credit card pays you interest on your deposit, but also charges interest when you use the card and maintain a balance from previous purchases. You can make purchases with this card as long as you stay within your limit/deposit. The purpose of using your

credit card is to establish a credit history, so make some small purchases but be sure to pay off your balance each month. Doing this
will show creditors that you're capable of responsibly handling your
credit and reflect a good payment history on your credit report.

MERCHANTS' ACCOUNTS

Merchants or retailers offer credit, and they are frequently excellent
sources to obtain your first line of credit. Merchants that generally
offer credit are appliance stores, furniture stores, jewelry stores, and
tire shops.

Prior to submitting an application, let the merchant know
that you've never had credit before, but that you're interested in
establishing an account with their store. The goal is to have your
efforts reported on your credit report, so find out if the merchant subscribes to one of the three major credit reporting agencies.

You'll need to make a purchase, so visit a shop that has something you can use. Ask the merchant if you may set up a ninety-day
account. If the merchant agrees to this, follow through, and make
all payments before the due date. The merchant will report good
payment patterns to the credit reporting agency.

To build up your credit report, you need to have two or three
active accounts that are being reported. Again, be diligent about
making timely payments. Once your report shows a good payment
history, apply for a major credit card, such as a Visa or a MasterCard.

HELP FROM A FRIEND OR RELATIVE

You can establish credit by having a relative or friend request a card
in your name from a creditor with which he already has an account.
Typically card issuers will allow a primary account holder to ask for

an additional card in another person's name. The primary cardholder is the one responsible for making the payments.

Sometimes, we may be reluctant to ask someone else to do us a favor, especially when it involves finances. One way to handle this particular situation is to let your relative or friend know that you're working on establishing credit. He will keep the card; you won't be using it. Your goal is to have a payment history on your credit report. Have your relative or friend ask the creditor to report the payment history to a credit reporting agency. After you've established your credit, your relative or friend can cancel this card. The cancellation will not be reflected on your record.

Obviously the friend or relative must be creditworthy and make payments on time. If he doesn't, your credit history may be jeopardized. That is why you want this to be a temporary thing.

CO-SIGNING

If you want to have a friend or relative co-sign for you, think about who you want to ask. Write their names in your journal. Also pencil in your objectives. When you approach them, let them know your goals and that you're aware of the risk they're taking and that once you have established new credit on your own the cosigned account will be closed. Be aware that co-signing is risky for the cosigner. Should you default on your payments, your friend or relative is responsible for paying off your bills. Negative entries will be reported on both accounts. Asking someone to co-sign for you is a serious favor. Don't make the mistake of treating it lightly.

DEPARTMENT STORE CARDS

The next step is to apply for a department store card. Again, make a few small purchases, and pay them off before the billing due date.

This way your credit report will show a solid payment pattern. Whatever you do, don't overextend your credit!

After three to six months, apply for a major credit card, such as a Visa or a MasterCard. Continue to maintain your credit habits, and limit yourself to only one or two cards.

Ideally you want to control your spending. If you have to stash your cards in a safe deposit box or freeze your credit cards in a block of ice, then do so.

Department store credit cards are not my favorite cards to keep. Their interest rates are much higher than those of most credit cards, and the temptation to use them more frequently is high.

Once you've established new credit with a good payment history, close the department store accounts and use only your low-interest Visa or MasterCard that you'll pay off each month. Most department stores take these cards, so why pay more?

PERSONAL SECURED OR SAVINGS PASSBOOK LOANS

Most banks offer a savings passbook loan that allows you to open a savings account on which you can draw interest. The deposit amount depends upon the minimum requirements of the bank and what you can afford. Some banks don't have a minimum limit, so in this case, put in $300 to $2,000.

After depositing the money, approach the bank for a loan against the deposit. You'll give the bank your savings passbook as collateral for the loan. Banks are amenable to this idea because the deposit covers any risk to them. If you fail to make payments on the loan, you will not have access to the account or any of the deposit money in it.

Because your goal is to build up your credit rating, follow a regular payment plan, and make all payments on time. The bank will report this to the credit reporting agency, which will record the information on your credit report. Repeat this process with a few other banks so that you have more than one good account on your report.

THE EQUAL CREDIT OPPORTUNITY ACT

The Equal Credit Opportunity Act was created to protect consumers against credit discrimination. The act states that you cannot be denied credit solely on the basis of being a woman. You also cannot be denied credit based upon whether you're single, married, separated, or divorced.

You can visit the Federal Trade Commission's Web site to review a text version of the act, or you can download your own copy at www.ftc.gov. If you have any questions, call the toll free number, 877-FTC-HELP.

As a woman making her way through the world of credit, you want to take steps to protect yourself. Here are some suggestions to help you do just that:

- You don't need to designate a Miss, Mrs., or Ms. when you apply for credit.

- It is inappropriate for creditors to query you about whether you want to have children someday.

- Creditors cannot assume that if you do have children, your income will drop.

- Creditors cannot ask you questions about birth control.

- All income, whether from full- or part-time employment, must be taken into consideration by a potential creditor. Child support and alimony are to be regarded as sources of income.

- You can choose whether you want to use your maiden name or your married name.

- You do not need your husband as a cosigner to open your own account provided you are considered creditworthy.

- Creditors cannot inquire about your husband's income unless your income is insufficient to qualify for credit. If you're applying jointly with your husband, or if he will be using the card and paying for the debts incurred, the creditor can ask for his information. Certain states have a community property law, and if you live in one of them, creditors can ask you about your husband's finances regardless. These states are Arizona, California, Idaho, Louisiana, Nevada, New Mexico, Texas, Washington, and Wisconsin.

In the event you feel you've been discriminated against due to your gender, contact the Federal Trade Commission and file a complaint. Some states have regional offices of the FTC. Check your local directory for the listing. Otherwise, try contacting the central office: Federal Trade Commission, Sixth & Pennsylvania Ave., NW, Washington, DC 20580; www.ftc.gov.

CREDIT IN YOUR LATER YEARS

If you're older and/or retired, there are some particular things you should know about credit. First of all, it's just as important that you have your own credit as it is for younger women. Many older women experience credit problems primarily because they currently have or had credit through their husbands. If you're authorized to use only your husband's card and he handles all the payments, you are without a credit history. Should anything happen to him, you will be in a precarious situation.

BE FAMILIAR WITH YOUR FINANCES

But take hope. With some thoughtful planning and strategic knowledge, you can fully understand what will happen to you when you grow older or your spouse dies. First, you need to know your rights. Under the federal Equal Credit Opportunity Act, or ECOA, you cannot be denied credit or have your current credit terminated on the basis of your age. A creditor cannot close your account or change the terms of a joint account due to the death of a spouse. A joint account is one for which both spouses apply and sign the credit agreement, so don't confuse this with an account for which your husband is the primary holder and you are listed as a user.

Should your spouse pass away, creditors may take some measures. They may ask to update your application or have you reapply; the latter holds especially true when the credit approval was granted due to your spouse's income, and they have reason to suspect you will be unable to support the current line of credit.

If you're asked to reapply, the creditors will determine whether they wish to continue with your credit, or they may adjust your limit to suit your present circumstances. A written response is mandatory, so you should expect a letter from the creditor within thirty days of your application. You may continue to use your credit without interruption during the time it takes for the application to be processed.

DENIAL OF A REAPPLICATION

If your application for credit is denied, the creditor must tell you the reason why. Most of the time, the original credit acceptance was based upon your spouse's income, and without it, your income doesn't appear to be enough to support the credit line.

To ensure some measure of protection in your retired years, know what kinds of credit you have. Briefly there are three types: (1) an individual account, (2) a joint account, and (3) a user account.

An *individual account* is opened under one person's name. The creditor has approved this account based upon that person's income and assets.

Two people open a *joint account*, generally a husband and a wife. Both people are held responsible for any debts charged; however, credit approval may be based upon either one income or both.

A *user account* is one where the primary holder was approved for credit but has been authorized to have another account card issued using a different name. The primary cardholder is held legally responsible for any and all debts incurred.

If you are uncertain about the types of accounts you have, contact your creditors, or request a copy of your credit report. The credit report will indicate the types of accounts.

WHEN A SPOUSE PASSES AWAY

Credit-wise, in the event of your spouse's death, the accounts that offer you some protection are an individual account in your own name and a joint account shared with your spouse. Anything else will be closed because of your partner's death. Having said this several times before, I'll repeat it again: it's best to have credit of your own, even if you share some joint accounts with your husband. This will protect you in case of emergency.

Every state has different community property laws pertaining to credit in the event of death. If you find yourself in a situation where your spouse has passed away and the creditors are trying to collect from you the balance on accounts that aren't in your name, contact an attorney.

JACKIE'S STORY

Jackie's husband died within the first year of their marriage. It was devastating enough to lose him so suddenly, but to make matters worse, the creditors were trying to force Jackie to pay off debt that was solely his, approximately $20,000 worth of credit card bills.

The creditors, demanding payment from Jackie, were making daily calls. She explained to them that she was not listed on his accounts.

When she contacted me, I referred her to an attorney to resolve this issue. Since Jackie had been married such a short time and the credit from her husband was established prior to the marriage in his name only, she was not liable for the debt. The attorney was able to resolve this issue with the creditors and allow Jackie to heal from her loss.

SHOULD YOU FEEL DISCRIMINATED AGAINST

If a creditor denies you credit and you have good reason to believe that you've been discriminated against, you can take some action. Review your rejection letter carefully. It's standard practice to include somewhere in the letter the appropriate federal agency to be contacted in case of a dispute. You may write this agency and tell your story. Include all the facts, verbal statements made, or discussions between you and the creditor. Attach any copies of correspondence documenting your case to support your letter to the agency.

WORKOUT

TRACKING YOUR CREDIT APPLICATIONS

Because you want to maintain control over your credit, you need to watch your progress when applying. In your journal note the type of account you applied for, such as individual, joint, or user. Then note the creditor information and the date you submitted the application.

WRAP-UP

Now that you've learned about the credit process, you're ready to apply. Make sure your financial goals are in place. It's far easier to control your spending and credit use than it is to overextend yourself and have to go through the process of rebuilding your credit.

Knowing your goals will help you plan for that rainy day or sudden emergency. No matter how overwhelming it feels when changes in your life occur, you'll feel far better falling back onto the financial security you've purposefully created.

COACH'S TIP

If you're married, keep track of your credit card account status. Make a list of all your cards and then note whether it's an individual account, a joint account, or a user account. That way, should anything happen—an emergency, divorce, or sudden death—you'll immediately know how to handle the various accounts.

9

REJECTION HURTS!

Rejections in life cause us to retreat and do nothing or move forward and get what we want. Most of us will experience a credit denial at some point in our lives. If you've recently experienced credit rejection, don't take it too personally. Don't think you're a "bad" person just because you received a denial letter. For the most part, there are standard reasons why a creditor will turn down an application, and we'll discuss what they are. Try to understand why you've been denied credit and then work on changing those issues into positives so that the next time you apply, you'll be approved.

REASONS FOR DENYING CREDIT

The most basic reason creditors will not extend credit is this: no credit history. To them, having no credit is the same as having bad credit. Creditors want to see a payment history on your credit report so they can evaluate your paying habits. You need to have at least two or three open lines of credit with a good payment history for a creditor to consider your application.

The most obvious reason creditors will reject someone's application is simply bad credit. If the negative or derogatory entries exceed the positive entries on a credit report, the creditor will flat-out deny the application. Negative entries include the following:

- Late payment. If you make your payment after the due date, it is considered late. However, it usually isn't reported as late if you make the payment before the following billing cycle.

- Delinquent account. An account is delinquent when it isn't paid on time.

- Charge-off. A charge-off occurs when the creditor determines it will not be able to collect the payments or balance. The creditor then charges the account off as a profit and loss, which is listed in your credit report.

- Collection account. A collection agency handles this account. The creditor has given up on the account and has sought outside help to collect.

- Repossession. A repossession occurs when an account is delinquent and the creditor feels it cannot collect. The item that is being financed is the security for the loan. If payments stop, the creditor will take the item back. If a creditor feels—in any way—that a person cannot maintain the payments, it will repossess the item.

- Foreclosure. A foreclosure usually occurs on a mortgage where the property is the security. If the payments fall behind, the creditor will initiate foreclosure proceedings to collect the past due payments or collect the full balance. If the creditor cannot collect the money within a specified time, the creditor will put the property up for a trustee sale.

- Judgment. A judgment involves a court action: someone sues you and wins the case against you. A judgment is money owed to the plaintiff. It is a public record.

- Tax lien. A tax lien is the result of the Internal Revenue Service or the state placing a lien on you to collect outstanding taxes. It is a public record.

- Bankruptcy. A bankruptcy is a public record filed with the court.

If your credit report reflects any of these items, you will need to rebuild your credit history. This will take some time and effort on your part, but there's no better time to begin this process than right now.

EXCESSIVE INQUIRIES

Without understanding how the credit system works, you are vulnerable to something that creditors do not look upon favorably, and that is excessive inquiries. For example, if you've been receiving a number of credit offers through the mail or via e-mail and you decide to reply to all of them, your credit report will reflect an excessive number of inquiries.

In addition, you are approaching credit all wrong. You are actually hurting yourself! A potential creditor who reviews your report will see all those inquiries but won't know whether you've been approved for them. It is common for a creditor who has approved your credit not to report the new credit on your credit report until you actually use the account. That is why a creditor looking at the report will see the inquiry and may assume you have unused credit that could cause you to become overextended. You'll wind up being denied the credit application.

OVEREXTENDED CREDIT

Overextended credit will cause a creditor to deny your application. When reviewing your credit report, creditors will calculate your debt to income ratio. They'll use the standard formula of your total debt divided by your gross monthly income (what you make before taxes) to figure what percentage of your gross monthly income is used to pay your debts. Certain percentages will trigger a credit denial, but essentially if your monthly income is low compared to your monthly expenses, a creditor will not extend you credit.

IF YOU ARE SELF-EMPLOYED

Many people work for themselves these days. However, if you're self-employed, creditors may see you as a potential credit risk. This is especially true if you've been self-employed for less than two years. The way each creditor handles this situation varies, so before you submit an application, it's a good idea to find out the creditor's criteria.

PUBLIC NOTICES

If you have been served the following public notices—bankruptcy, judgements, or tax liens—a creditor will turn down your application. Credit reporting agencies keep tabs on anything reported with the county recorder's office. If the item reported appears negative, a creditor will make note of it and reject your application outright.

If you're denied credit, the creditor must send you a letter letting you know within thirty days of turning down your application. When you receive this letter, you can obtain a free copy of your credit report from the credit reporting agency listed on the letter. You must make this request within sixty days of being denied the credit.

WRAP-UP

Obtaining credit takes careful planning and preparation, so don't feel bad if you receive a denial letter in the mail. Determine why you've been turned down, and then put your energy into changing your situation so that you can be approved for credit.

Do your homework. Review your credit report so that you know what the creditor is looking at. Contact the creditor prior to submitting an application to learn about its terms for granting credit. Maintain solid financial habits, such as paying your accounts on time, reviewing your credit report for inaccuracies, and controlling your spending. All of these measures will help you avoid being denied credit in the future.

COACH'S TIP

If being turned down for credit strikes an emotional chord within you or causes you to feel like giving up on your new financial fitness plan, don't let it. Be patient with yourself. There is an art to credit application, and you can master it.

10

FACING THE HURDLES

———

Bills and more bills! We all have them. The scary part is when there are more bills than money. It's easy to think that no one knows the financial troubles you're facing. But let me tell you, I've had my days of more bills than money to pay them with. I hope parts of my story will show you that you can face your financial troubles and overcome them, given faith, a plan, and time.

I remember only too well the year we sold our real estate company to reinvest in another company that never got off the ground. Our income was cut 70 percent. When you're living a lifestyle that is higher than your income, it's time for a reality check. It doesn't happen overnight. Although our income dropped, the bills remained the same.

I felt helpless, disorganized, and totally out of control; I was devastated. Scrambling around for the next dollar just to survive became next to impossible. It was time to get a game plan together. I knew I couldn't make everyone happy, so I devised a plan that was workable for our family. The first thing I did was to see where our money was going and what was coming in.

If you ever feel disorganized, are behind on your payments, or have no idea where your money goes, I strongly recommend coming up with a household game plan.

First, gather all your monthly bills and your pay stubs for the month, along with any other related paperwork. You'll need some paper and a calculator. Next, total the monthly income. Then, calculate how much money you spend each month. Write these numbers down and keep them handy.

Now, keep track of all the money you spend. You may want to purchase an inexpensive memo pad to carry with you and record every penny you spend. If you go to the ATM machine, jot that down, and itemize each payment you make. You may spend an entire $20 in a matter of minutes without really knowing where it all went.

Do the same thing when you visit the supermarket. Break down all of your costs. Do you buy coffee every morning? How many times a week? How much are you paying per cup? What about sodas from a vending machine? Write it down. The idea is to track *everything*. Only then will you know where your money is going.

WARNING!

At first you may think that keeping track of your spending is a hassle. However, it's one of the best money management tools you can implement. When I began to do this exercise, I couldn't believe how much money I was spending on things that we could live without. Knowing exactly where your money goes actually helps you control its flow and pay your bills; it even helps you save money.

YOUR THIRTY-DAY EXPENSE JOURNAL

At the end of the month, examine where your money went. You'll be surprised at the figures. Little things like coffee, snacks, and magazines can quickly add up to $15 or $20 a week, or a monthly $60 or $80. But the point isn't to beat yourself up over where your money went; it's to figure out where you can cut back.

For instance, if you frequently eat out, you can significantly reduce your food budget by brown bagging some of your meals. Getting an overall picture of how you spend money allows you to take control of your finances.

PRIORITIZING

When faced with personal financial disaster, I finally realized that I had lost focus on what bills needed to be paid first. So many bill collectors were calling and demanding payment that I would pay one bill, neglecting another one. One day it dawned on me that the bill collectors yelling the loudest weren't the ones who needed to be paid first. My priority was to make sure there was food on the table, the utilities were paid, and the house payment was made on time. These survival expenses became the foundation of my game plan.

ESSENTIALS AND NONESSENTIALS

Once I realized that survival was the most important thing, I compiled a list of our essential and nonessential bills. Some of the things on the essential list were easy to write down, such as food, shelter, and utilities; other things were debatable and needed more thought.

Look at the list of your expenses, and determine which ones are essential or absolutely necessary to your day-to-day survival. Continue breaking down your bills in this manner. What is the next level of bills? Car insurance, medical insurance, medical needs, child support, and loans for automobiles are critical. A good rule of thumb for this secondary category is any credit or item purchased with a secured loan or with collateral. (A secured loan is one in which the item purchased with credit is used as collateral. If payments are not made, the item is repossessed.)

Now, review the remaining bills. These are probably all nonessential bills, in other words, debts that have no immediate consequences in your life (other than vanity or comfort). Remove these bills from your life. Credit and charge cards, attorney bills, and news and magazine subscriptions are all nonessential expenses. Pay these bills only after you have paid your essential bills.

BORDERLINE BILLS

You may have some bills left that don't seem to fall into either category. Examine these bills more carefully. The debt will fit into one category or the other. Generally costs such as private schools, day care, clothing, health clubs or gyms, and life insurance are the expenses that can cause some confusion.

Most borderline bills are luxuries and extras. If there are ways to minimize these costs, do so. Otherwise, you'll need to decide the value of an expense and the degree to which it is an essential or nonessential debt in your life. Borderline debts may be ones you need to give up.

I am *not* saying that you should avoid paying your bills. If you're struggling to make ends meet, pay the essential bills first, and then pay the others when you have the money.

CAUTION!

One of the dumbest decisions I made when prioritizing my bills was giving up our medical insurance. Everyone in my family seemed healthy, so I decided that we could temporarily live without medical insurance.

A month after our medical insurance lapsed, our daughter, Mindy, had to have emergency brain surgery. She was diagnosed with hydrocephalus—a blockage in a ventricle in her brain that caused fluid to build up. Her brain had swelled due to fluid pressure. Mindy slipped into a coma and was near death.

The neurosurgeon didn't know whether Mindy would survive the surgery. He had to insert a shunt in her brain and relieve the fluid pressure. We were sent to the chapel to pray and wait.

You can't imagine my panic and fear. We could possibly lose Mindy, and we had no medical insurance! I was afraid the hospital wouldn't help us once the administrators realized we had no insurance coverage. But I was wrong. The hospital brought in the best doctors and specialists to help our daughter.

In the chapel we prayed for Mindy. Family and friends came and prayed for her as well. I knew God was with us.

Well, Mindy survived the procedure. We discovered that she had been born with a congenital condition that took fourteen years to surface. We were so thankful to see her progress, and the surgery appeared to be a success. But the hospital bill was still looming over our heads. The surgery cost more than $50,000. Without medical insurance I was afraid we would have to file for bankruptcy.

We met with a woman who indicated that Mindy's emergency was a trauma case. The hospital had special programs for children diagnosed with her condition. We still had to pay a deductible, but that seemed small in comparison to the entire cost. Our daughter is alive today, and not a day goes by that I don't think about how blessed we are to have her with us.

I caution you once again: use care in deciding which bills to give up. Making the wrong decision can come back to haunt you.

WHY PRIORITIZE?

Prioritizing your bills will show you where money needs to be allocated. Using the amount of your monthly income, you should now be able to figure not only what you have, but also where it's most needed. These are the bills that will get paid first. Pay them on time. If you're having problems paying your bills, determining your essentials will mean that your basic life requirements are met. The point of all of these exercises is to help you take control of your finances and get into the habit of paying the survival expenses first.

STILL OVERWHELMED BY YOUR BILLS?

If after reading all this, you still feel completely overwhelmed by your bills and expenses, it might be a good idea for you to seek outside help. This is especially true when you have more bills than income, and you realize that you don't have enough income to make a dent in paying off your debt. I suggest that you speak with a debt management company that can help you get a grip on your situation and understand your options. You may contact Cambridge Credit Counseling Corporation at 800-897-2200, ext. 758.

WORKOUT

TRACKING YOUR CASH EXPENDITURES

Keep a list of your cash expenditures for thirty days. Remember to write down everything! Include the date, the amount, and the category; for example, July 25, 2001, $5.75 for fast food and $32.17 for clothing. Tally your totals after the thirty days are up.

TRACKING YOUR CREDIT CARD EXPENDITURES

Log all of your credit card transactions for thirty days. Make sure you jot down each expense, and separate these expenses by categories; include the date and the merchant.

WRAP-UP

Many women may feel that they have too much debt and not enough savings. This is true of most people. The trick to controlling your money, so it doesn't control you, is to look at where you've been so that you can get ahead. Learn from your mistakes.

Organize your bills, and then prioritize them. Work on changing old money habits that don't work or produce the financial results you desire. Learn to tame the instant gratification urge. Allow yourself time to make these changes. Make improvements slowly but surely.

More than anything else, deciding to do something about your finances and then acting on that decision is the key to attaining financial security. Once you have your plan in place, things will eventually change.

COACH'S TIP

Consider your household game plan as your new financial routine. Refer to your plan often. Give it time to succeed. Recognize the small victories, and don't give up!

11

YOUR
FITNESS PLAN

For any type of fitness program, you must set goals. This is especially true with your money and finances.

Used wisely, credit can be a terrific financial tool. Unfortunately too many of us use credit for all the wrong reasons. We may purchase items on impulse, or buy things we can't really afford, or maintain a lifestyle that is way beyond our current income. Used in this manner, credit becomes a nemesis, eventually undermining our financial security.

But there is such a thing as good debt, and in this chapter, we'll talk about how to set credit and financial goals so that you are able to manage your debt responsibly and wisely.

So how do you avoid being overwhelmed by credit? All you need to do to put a game plan in place is determine your short- and long-term financial goals. By setting goals, you'll be able to progress step by step and eventually attain what you want. This, in turn, enhances your sense of confidence, allowing you to create new goals and achieve them.

THE ADVANTAGES OF CREDIT

Credit, be it a mortgage or an equity loan, can help you buy or refinance a home. A line of credit can enable you to start up a business. You can use credit to fund a college education. More often than not, you need credit to purchase a car, motor vehicle, or boat. You can use credit for material things, such as retail items, travel, and entertainment. You can be advanced cash based upon your credit limit. All of these advantages can be helpful to you at one time or another.

PURCHASING A HOME

Buying a home is often referred to as the American dream, but the idea of making such a large purchase can be overwhelming. Through the extension of credit, you can make the dream of owning a home come true. To qualify for a home mortgage or an equity line of credit, you must have a good credit history. Establish solid payment patterns, and when the time comes for you to buy your home, you'll be regarded as creditworthy.

There's another reason to have an excellent credit history: a good credit rating will help you to qualify for the best interest rates and terms. If your history has some problems, you may be charged higher rates, or you may not be extended credit at all. You cannot qualify for a mortgage or equity loan without credit, so it pays to manage your credit wisely.

Having credit doesn't mean that you need to be in debt. In fact, a mortgage is considered good credit because you're building future equity. Your home becomes an asset. As the mortgage balance decreases, the property values increase. The trick is that you purchased something that will retain its value in the long run.

BUSINESS CREDIT

There has been tremendous growth in the number of small businesses. The good news is that 50 percent of small businesses are
owned by women. If you're considering following suit, you're going
to need credit. You may use it to get the business up and running,
to make improvements, or to be a backup reserve to handle unforeseen problems.

Let's say you want to get a loan from a bank to start up a business. To obtain the bank's approval, you'll need a good payment history reflected on your credit report. Many businesses have been
started with a credit card. If you need your credit card for your business expenses, ask your creditor to increase the amount on your line
of credit. Ensure that your account is in good standing and that
you've been making your payments on time. Pay off the balance as
soon as possible.

CREDIT FOR AUTOMOBILES,
MOTOR VEHICLES, OR BOATS

At some point in your life, you will purchase a car, and you will be glad
you have established a good credit history. Still even if you've never had
credit before, or if you've had bad credit, some companies will allow
you to establish credit. But you'll end up with higher interest rates,
and the cost of the loan will be significantly higher in most instances.

Since an automobile is a big-ticket item, probably second to buying a home, the ideal is to be able to pay cash for it. If you can't pay
fully in cash, then make as large a down payment as you can. Strive
to pay the loan off as soon as possible by making larger monthly payments than your monthly minimum. Review your contract to make
sure there are no prepayment penalties.

STUDENT LOANS

With the rising cost of education, many students have turned to loans to finance their schooling. Banks and universities offer financial aid packages. A number of student loans are financed through the government. Students are loaned the money, but payment is deferred until after they're out of school. For the most part, interest rates are low. You still have to qualify for assistance, so again, you'll want established credit with a history of good payments.

MATERIAL GOODS

This category tempts most people to fall heavily into debt. Many people seek to establish credit through major credit cards, along with charge cards from department stores, retail shops, airlines, and entertainment companies. This is what I call credit for material gain.

More often than not, people use their cards to buy something today that they think they can pay off later. Some purchases can be necessities, such as a major appliance. However, have a plan in place to keep from overspending.

Remember that you want credit; you don't want excessive debt. By using your credit wisely and not succumbing to the impulse purchase or the latest fashion, you'll establish and maintain a good credit history. Avoid becoming overextended, make your payments on time, and pay off your accounts as soon as you can. This way, you can avoid being denied credit in the future. Always plan ahead, and have credit set aside for an emergency as well.

CASH LOANS

Many people use cash from a line of credit to pay off other debts, such as taking out a loan so that they can consolidate their payments and get a lower interest rate. Or they'll start up a business, pay for travel, or buy personal items or other things using a cash loan. If you take out such a loan from a bank, you still need to qualify for it. Having a good credit report and paying off the loan responsibly are critical.

GETTING OUT OF DEBT

If you're already in debt, then make it your goal to get out of it. The end result of your efforts will be a cleaned-up credit report and a newfound sense of creditworthiness. Write down your goal. Then think about how long it will take to attain your goal.

What's the best way to bring your debt down? Come up with a plan, then stick to it. Be consistent and methodical. If you pay off one account, take the extra money and apply it to another. If you require more motivation than a zero balance, have a long-term goal, such as buying a car, that inspires you to put the effort into paying down your present debt.

START SAVING

Want to start saving, but just can't seem to get around to it? Sit down with your budget, and determine how much you can set aside each week or month. Don't just think about saving; figure out how to make it happen. If it's possible, have a certain amount automatically deducted from your paycheck and deposited into a savings account. Or when it is time to pay your bills, pay yourself first. Fill out the savings deposit form, and place it on top of your bills.

Start out with an amount you can reach. For instance, you determine that you can put aside $100 a month. In one year you'll wind up with $1,200 without interest. Focus on the end result.

Once you achieve that goal, come up with another amount, then strive to reach that.

RETIREMENT GOALS

It's never too early to set retirement goals. You may want to start by reading up on retirement plans. Can you take advantage of an employer's 401(k) program? Perhaps you can open an IRA account. Research all of your options. Then decide where you want to start. As with savings, you can have a specified amount deducted from your paycheck and put into a retirement fund.

You may want to seek professional advice about investment programs. Familiarize yourself with stocks, bonds, and mutual funds. You will need to save a considerable sum, so use worksheets and projections to establish an overall goal and then break this goal down into monthly and yearly objectives.

GOAL SETTING

We've talked a little bit about establishing goals. Let's take a moment to think about what a goal really is. It's the end result of a desire into which you've directed energy and effort. People often go through life responding to the events that occur around them, not realizing or achieving what they really want. Determining what you want is often the hardest part of setting goals.

The best way to approach goal setting is to make a list of what you want. Do you want a house, a car, a boat, a student loan, or a credit card? Do you want to be debt free? How about having savings or a nice retirement account? Maybe you've had credit problems in the past, and now you need to strategize about rebuilding it.

Review what you've put on your list and think about how you

can make it happen. Prioritize your desires. You can accomplish your goals by planning what to do and then taking action. It may take a while, but slowly and surely you'll reach your goal.

I've found that once you start implementing goals, the easier it is to follow through. Goal setting can decrease the overwhelming aspects of what you want to do because you know where you want to go, and it's just a matter of focusing on the right direction. Tracking your progress can be a big confidence booster as you see what you can accomplish when you put your mind to it.

At first you'll need to set aside some time to really consider your goals and how you want to achieve them. There may be some homework involved. Research is just another way to put energy into your project. By being able to break each goal down into realistic steps, the easier it will be to follow through. With credit, carefully plan how you'll use it and how to maintain it.

DETERMINING YOUR NEEDS

When you set credit goals, decide where you specifically want assistance. For example, you may be interested in buying a car. In addition to researching the best car for your needs, shop around for the best deals. Having established credit that shows you're responsible with your finances will make this task easier. Don't set yourself up for defeat, however, by wanting a grandiose or luxury vehicle. Stay within your means. Good credit is affordable. Having monthly payments that are too high for you is bad use of credit.

If you're not ready to make a large purchase but want to establish credit, list the number of credit cards you want along with their limit amounts. Again, make sure that your income can support any purchases you may make using credit. Above all, avoid overextending yourself. If you have a few open lines of credit with zero balances, that's great. When you do buy something, pay it off as quickly as you can. That way, should you need to qualify for more credit, your past credit history will look good.

PLANNING FOR YOUR FUTURE

In planning for your future, you'll find it helpful to have both short- and long-term credit goals. Think of the short-term goals as stepping-stones to the larger ones. For instance, a short-term goal could be making your monthly payments on time. Your action is setting aside a regular time to pay your bills and then following through with that commitment. An added bonus: you won't waste any time worrying about whether your payments are late. Plus, you're building a solid credit history—something you'll live with for the rest of your life.

Setting aside money each month in savings will help you reach your long-term goal for retirement. Being debt free is also a step toward saving for your retirement. A long-term goal could be buying a house or a car. Achieving your short-term goal of paying your bills on time helps you attain the long-term goal of making a large purchase by showing that you are creditworthy.

TEN STEPS TO HELP YOU SET YOUR GOALS

1. Write your goals on a sheet of paper. Keep it handy so you can refer to it often.

2. Visualize. Picture attaining your goal. Cut out a picture of whatever you desire: a house, a car, or an appliance. Hang the picture in a place where you'll see it.

3. Come up with a realistic time frame to achieve your goal. It may take you several months to obtain certain types of

credit or savings, so give yourself the time you need to be successful.

4. Write out your action plan. If you're applying for credit cards, list the firms you want to contact, and list the type of credit you want to obtain. If it's a cash purchase, make a plan about how you will begin saving. If it's a home purchase, plan how you'll save for your down payment. If it's for retirement, write a plan on how much you need to save.

5. Don't let other things take the place of your goal. Setting aside time to follow through with your plan of action is critical. Don't make excuses for not following through.

6. Think about things that could forestall your plans. For example, if you're getting ready to apply for a line of credit and you notice an error on your credit report, deal with the error now. Be sure it is corrected before making your application.

7. Know your motives. Are you working on building your credit for the future? Or are you just trying to get material things for immediate use? If it's only for the latter, you'll be better off not obtaining credit.

8. Learn from your past experiences.

9. Believe in yourself. Believe in your plan. If things don't turn out exactly as you planned, examine why they worked out the way they did. Don't dwell on your "mistakes." Learn from them and correct them instead. Next time around, you'll know better.

10. Take action. Do the little steps first. Proceed from step to step. Rather than worry about what needs to get done, just start doing it.

WRAP-UP

Identifying what you need to do so your plan is successful can save you time and money. By breaking down what you want to accomplish into attainable steps, you will make progress. Remember, it's far easier to accomplish something with a plan.

You must know how the credit and financial systems work and what you need to do to build a successful credit and financial portfolio. Armed with this knowledge, you can increase your chances of being approved for credit and getting a savings plan in order. In the long run, being creditworthy and financially savvy will give you greater opportunity to make money and gain financial security.

COACH'S TIP

If you have a tendency to procrastinate, tell yourself that putting something off only delays the consequences. As you take small steps to achieve a goal, you'll realize that procrastination is simply a habit. You can choose to practice it or not. It's your choice.

12

LOVE AND MONEY

———

You're in love. You've set a wedding date, and you have so much to think about, so many plans to make. There's one topic, however, that probably won't be discussed. And yet this topic will affect the two of you for the rest of your lives. In fact, more couples argue about this than any other topic. If you haven't guessed it by now, the topic is finances. Money issues in many cases are just not part of the happily ever after story, but they should be.

Before you marry, it's a good idea to sit down and discuss the financial future the two of you envision as a couple. Why? Because after you're wed, you'll need to talk about money on a regular basis.

Rather than wait for issues to arise, begin a pattern of discussing things openly and rationally. You'll find out where the two of you might have different ideas about how the finances should be handled. Such differences aren't the end of the world: They are just something the two of you need to resolve together. You should talk about your net worth, your credit ratings, your financial goals, whether you want children, the cost of raising children and your family money traditions.

Set aside time to discuss these matters. Start off by listening to each other. Be patient, and allow each other to fully explain the situation. It will take understanding and respect to work through each of these subjects with your fiancé.

NET WORTH

It's probably best to tackle one issue at a time. Let's start with a net worth statement, which is essentially an overview of your financial situation. If you sold off all of your assets and paid off all of your debts, you'd have your net worth.

The two of you should draw up your net worth statements separately. If money is a really big deal, you may want to fully disclose all of your assets and liabilities through a prenuptial agreement. But I'm going to assume that your situation is fairly low key. Look over your net worth statements together. Think in terms of questions rather than criticisms.

What if one partner has a negative net worth? Better to learn about that now rather than after the marriage. Ultimately the two of you will have to reach your own decisions, but take a good look at the numbers. What seems to be a problem could be something else. Don't rush to any conclusions. Maybe your fiancé just completed graduate school and has a number of student loans that need to be paid off. The degree will probably translate into a higher-paying position, which could be a positive in the long run. But if there are problems with excessive credit debt, there could be deep financial trouble ahead. Now is the time to come up with a mutually satisfying resolution to handle such issues.

CREDIT RATINGS

Which brings us to credit ratings. This matter will definitely affect your future plans, from buying a house, furniture, major appliances, or cars, to having children and raising a family. It's probably easiest to share copies of your credit report. You'll be able to glean a lot about your partner's financial habits by reviewing their credit history. Does he carry a lot of debt? Does he pay his accounts on time? Does he have a history of negative payment patterns? The two of you should also review your reports for inaccuracies too.

MONICA AND PHIL'S STORY

When I was speaking at a conference in Georgia, Monica and Phil wanted to talk to me. They were getting married and wanted me to review their credit reports together.

Phil's credit report was spotless. It was great. On the other hand, Monica's credit report had serious problems. There were numerous accounts that had been paid late and even some collection accounts. Several years earlier, Monica had lost her job and fell behind on paying her bills. She thought since she had caught up with the past due payments, her credit report would be in good shape. She was definitely wrong and had never requested a copy of her credit report until then.

Phil was stunned. He didn't realize the baggage Monica was bringing into their finances. After we put a game plan together for them, Phil felt better, knowing there were solutions to this problem. The wedding was still on.

If one partner has bad debt, how will that affect the other once you're married? Well, you'll have to decide how to rectify that situation, whether the credit risk partner comes up with a repayment plan and rebuilds the credit or you decide not to share a joint account. If you choose the latter, you will face difficulties when you want to make a joint purchase, such as a house. One spouse's negative credit rating will mean higher interest rates or potentially a smaller loan offer. And not pooling any of your resources could put a strain on the marriage.

CREDIT CARDS FOR TWO

While going over your reports, you'll want to talk specifically about credit cards. Will you share a joint account? How many will you have? What limits will be set? Will you pay them off each month? One strategy that many successful couples have used is to opt for separate cards. It costs more for the separate memberships or annual fees, but the family credit doesn't get ruined should one partner charge irresponsibly. Or you may wish to share one or two joint cards designated for household expenses and have separate cards for personal costs. Again, if one partner has too much credit card debt, will the two of you mutually assume paying that off? As a couple, you may want to join forces and bring that debt down together.

FINANCIAL GOALS

You don't want to let money matters separate you. Rather, you want to learn to work together. You'll need this team attitude throughout your married life. One way you can solidly build your future is by talking about what you want. What are your financial goals?

Each of you should make a list of the things you want: a house, vacations, no debt, budgets, and so on. Discuss the type of retirement you wish to have. Don't overlook matters such as employment—outlining the perfect career, eventually starting one's own business, attaining a certain level of accomplishment, or being a stay-at-home mom. A lot of these dreams or goals will require financial planning to make them happen.

Ask each other about opinions regarding how to handle the finances. What kind of budget limits do you want to establish? Will you have a joint or separate checking account? Some couples have both, reserving the joint account for household expenses and the other for personal ones.

What standards do you have regarding the cost of an item? For example, what's a reasonable expenditure for clothes, dining out, entertainment, vacations, gifts, and the like? You don't need exact numbers; a good estimate will do.

Who will pay the bills? Will you track them jointly so that the responsibility is shared? Do you plan to set aside time each month to go over the progress of your financial plans? How will you organize your financial paperwork, and where will important papers be kept? And how much can one spouse spend without consulting the other? A lot of seemingly small details can prove crucial after your money matters are merged.

INVESTMENTS

Investments are a good way to grow your money. As a newly married couple, you are wise to consider your investment options, especially for your retirement years. Saving for investments should be a part of your budget, so you'll need to know how much to allot for this. You'll also need to take into consideration the other's investment expectations. He may want to invest in some high-risk technology stocks, and she may prefer a more conservative approach, such as a savings account, CDs, or money market accounts. Ideally your investment portfolio should be a combination of these two approaches. The two of you may want to seek financial planning advice to cover all of your financial bases and come up with a plan that takes all of your goals into consideration.

WHAT ABOUT KIDS?

This one you've probably talked about, but have you discussed the cost of having children? Right now, you can figure that it will take approximately $200,000 to raise one child. That's a lot of money.

Once you have children, will both of you continue to work? What type of childcare arrangements will you make? Do either of you work for a company that has good family care benefits? If both work and an emergency arises, you'll need to figure out who will handle the situation. Certain factors can help you with some of these decisions. For instance, the spouse with the more flexible schedule should probably be the one who's on call for emergencies.

Then there's the question of college. Do both feel that parents should pay for the entirety of their child's college tuition? How will you save for such costs? That will need to be implemented into your budget now.

What about allowances? How do you intend to teach your kids about finances? You have a lot to talk about in this category.

FAMILY MONEY TRADITIONS

How you were raised with money influences how you deal with your finances. Talking about your upbringing can be very informative and helpful. Maybe one of you grew up in a very thrifty and financially disciplined household. This could have ramifications if the other was raised with a parent who was a zealous overspender. Just because a parent acted one way doesn't guarantee that a child will follow suit.

Perhaps finances were never openly talked about in your family; you may feel uncomfortable discussing such matters. Understanding this and then sharing the reasons why it's important to mutually deal with money matters can help you amicably resolve this family money tradition.

This talk can also reveal certain attitudes that one may have toward money. Perhaps his family has a money tradition of lavishing gifts upon the other whenever a birthday or holiday occasion arises. He may expect reciprocal behavior, but you come from a family that modestly exchanges gifts. His feelings get hurt, you complain about the amount of money he spends, and you fight.

Knowing about these traditions and family influences can help both partners by examining expectations. It's safe to say that there will be differences between the two of you, but the key is to communicate with each other and come up with reasonable resolutions.

TALK ABOUT IT

At first talking about all these money matters may be awkward, but it's good to discuss these things rather than avoid them until a crisis comes up. It will also get easier and more comfortable to reveal your money concerns, because you've created a safe and rational arena to talk about them. There is a positive note to these discussions too. Deciding how to unite your financial forces can result in smart money management benefiting both in the long run.

Spend more time focusing on how to make your money work for you instead of fighting over who's to blame for this or that problem. Address concerns and potential problems as they arise. By knowing what your goals are and how you intend to accomplish them, you've set up a proactive financial approach to your future as a couple. Now you can focus on tracking your progress and reassessing your needs as you achieve those short- and long- term goals together.

D-I-V-O-R-C-E

The two of you have decided that you'd be better off divorced. So what happens financially when the marriage ends? Now there's a topic no one wants to discuss! However, if you and your spouse are parting ways, there are a few things you should know. First, get legal counsel. Don't rely on others to ensure your financial security. It's very important that you take care of your own interests. Consider these realities:

- Twenty-eight percent of women will actually receive some kind of financial support from their ex-husbands.

- For women awarded child support or alimony payments, more than one-third will not receive these funds.

- Your lifestyle will be dramatically affected. Most women experience a 30 to 45 percent drop in income.

- Go out and get yourself a good attorney, one who specializes in matrimonial law. You want someone who knows all the ins and outs of divorce proceedings.

Next, it's time to close all the joint accounts. Before you cancel all the credit cards, however, have credit in your own name. If you don't have your own card, apply for one right away! Once that's set, contact all of the creditors and close the joint accounts. Let them know about the divorce. If your ex is responsible for certain debts, tell them. Ask if they'll inform you when he is delinquent with payments or defaults on the account. Protect your credit throughout this transition. Review your credit reports to make sure no late payments are being reported.

Properly deal with all other shared assets. If you share a car, change the registration. The same goes for any savings, investments, or other assets owned jointly. If the two of you have a broker, inform him about the divorce. Ask the broker to contact you regarding transactions that don't have your approval. This is especially true if you share a margin account (one where the money used to purchase an investment is really a loan from the brokerage firm). Otherwise, you could end up liable for both the loan and the interest. If you have a will, update it at this time too.

You could be entitled to receive part of your ex's retirement benefits if they were earned during the marriage. For instance, your ex-husband had a 401(k) plan to which he actively contributed. An attorney can petition the court for what's called a qualified domestic relations order (QDRO). It's possible that the judge could award you with a one-time payment, a lump sum payment, or upon retirement, multiple pension payments. If it is granted, you can put your portion into an IRA. Don't pass up this opportunity for retirement money.

If you've been married ten years or more, you may qualify for Social Security benefits based on your ex's wages. Get professional advice on this one because certain requirements must be met. If you meet them, you may be entitled to receive benefits that won't affect what he'd receive.

KEEP YOURSELF ORGANIZED

Keep notes about all your finances. If you have the kids, track their costs, and maintain accurate records. You need to know the real cost of raising the kids. You can also compare it with what you actually get from your ex. Likewise, if your ex is frequently late with the payments, doesn't give you the right amount, or doesn't make the payments at all, you have records. Should you need to take the matter to court, you're prepared.

Also, keep all of your paperwork together and organized. Documents, such as your divorce decree and settlement papers, alimony and child support agreements, and property settlements should be in one place. Make copies and put the originals in a secure place such as a safe deposit box. Give copies to your lawyer.

WRAP-UP

The message of this chapter is to protect yourself financially! Whether you're in love or your marriage ties are broken, you need to look out for your own financial interests. This doesn't mean you can't fairly and amicably work things out with your spouse. It does mean that you actively take part in financial discussions. It also means that you know how to manage your finances. Genuine financial security requires you to think, save, and communicate.

COACH'S TIP

When you're looking for an attorney, ask friends and family who have been through a divorce to recommend someone. If you're having trouble finding legal representation, you can contact the American Academy of Matrimonial Lawyers (www.aaml.org) for listings in your area.

13

I'M THROWING IN THE TOWEL: BANKRUPTCY

———

What do you do if you're facing serious debt? Maybe you've been desperately juggling your bills but getting nowhere. Perhaps you suddenly find yourself in dire straits: your ability to pay back your debt is interrupted by job loss or severely compromised due to an emergency, and you have no financial reserves to fall back on. You're so overwhelmed that you begin to think bankruptcy is your only way out of this mess. Many people file for bankruptcy because they can't handle creditors' harassment.

Before you declare bankruptcy, you must fully understand the consequences of that decision. Don't even think about bankruptcy until you have seriously looked at all the other options available to you. Contacting a credit counseling company should always be your first choice before filing for bankruptcy. Sometimes it's possible to restructure your debt so that you can manage it. You may be able to rewrite your loans and work with a nonprofit credit counseling company that handles debt consolidation.

Often people think of bankruptcy as an easy way out. That is not the case. You should think about bankruptcy only as a last-chance solution. Let's briefly consider your other options before we discuss bankruptcy.

REWRITING YOUR LOANS

This action involves contacting your creditors and asking them to do two things: (1) extend the time you have to repay the debt, and (2) change the monthly payment to an amount you can actually afford. Don't make the mistake of automatically thinking that creditors will refuse this request. Remember they're in the business of extending credit. Because the length of your loan is now longer and the payments smaller, they will make money off your situation. However, preserving your credit record is important and worth the effort it may take to ensure you remain in good standing.

Consequently if you can retain a good credit history, you should do so. When you are able to get back on your feet and have your finances under control, contact the creditors again. This time, restructure the loan for a shorter term and make higher payments; just make sure that you can afford the modified terms. The rule of thumb is, the faster you can pay off a debt, the less money you spend in the long run. And if you can avoid carrying debt from month to month, do so by paying off any balances as soon as you can.

When you negotiate with a creditor, never offer to pay something that you can't afford. Make your offer affordable to you.

NONPROFIT CREDIT COUNSELORS

Almost every city has credit counselors who will assist you with your debt issues. Some will review all of your finances, both income and debt, for a small fee. They will then counsel you on how to work out your debts for yourself. If your situation is rather complicated, they can help by establishing a repayment program for you. In this instance they will contact your creditors, advising them of your particular situation, your work with a credit counselor, and any pertinent details about your repayment program.

Once your creditors have been notified and have accepted the proposed repayment plan, you'll make fixed payments to a personal trust fund. This payment is used to repay all of your creditors until the debts are reconciled. Repayment programs are prorated and can take up to three to six years to complete. At any time during the repayment period, should you have questions or problems arise, a counselor is available to speak with you.

When you have completed the repayment program, your credit report will be updated. Order copies of all three reports so that you can ensure the information is accurate.

STILL CONSIDERING BANKRUPTCY?

If none of the aforementioned options is viable for you, and you're still considering bankruptcy, then carefully think about the following:

- Declaring bankruptcy will not clear your credit record.

- A bankruptcy *does* appear on your record (as a public notice).

- Bankruptcy is considered negative information by creditors and can significantly deter your efforts to obtain new credit.

- Some employers and companies may not hire individuals who have filed for bankruptcy.

- Bankruptcy information can stay on your credit report up to ten years.

The point of all this information is to make you aware of the consequences of declaring bankruptcy.

Sometimes people think bankruptcy will dissolve all their money cares. To some extent, it does, but there is a price to be paid. If you are in serious financial trouble or if it will take you more than five years to pay off your current debt, get help. Contact a credit counseling company. Read a few books about bankruptcy, and talk with a bankruptcy attorney. At the very least, take some sort of action rather than postpone dealing with your debt situation.

HOW DOES BANKRUPTCY WORK?

Known as the solution of last resort, bankruptcy is a last-ditch legal effort to hold off total financial disaster. There are three types of bankruptcy: Chapter 7, Chapter 11, and Chapter 13. In essence each chapter follows a standard procedure.

THE PROCESS

Step 1: A petition is filed with a federal or state court. This petition states that you are insolvent. That is, you have no means (income or assets) to pay off your debts.

Step 2: A repayment program is negotiated with the court and your creditors if applicable.

Step 3: You are granted a discharge. Your debts are settled, typically for less than their full amount.

THE PROS AND CONS OF BANKRUPTCY

As with most things, there are pros and cons to the bankruptcy process. What are some of the pros? Well, filing for bankruptcy gives you legal protection from your creditors. It also settles most of your debts while preventing the loss of your home (if you're an owner). Bankruptcy may provide protection against the IRS should the agency attempt to seize your property for back taxes. And it offers you a chance to start all over again.

In addition to some of the things I've already mentioned, there are cons to declaring bankruptcy. For one, you lose your financial privacy. You become involved with the courts. In some instances not all debts are resolved. You lose any assets you may have to help pay off your debt. And of course, your credit history is seriously damaged.

TYPES OF BANKRUPTCY

As I've mentioned, there are three types of bankruptcy. Our brief discussion will help you familiarize yourself with Chapters 7 and 13; Chapter 11 pertains to businesses. You can qualify for Chapter 11 only if you are a business or if your debt is greater than the maximum amount allowed in a Chapter 13 bankruptcy. Bankruptcy laws are changing, and filing for a Chapter 7 may become harder to do. Credit counseling may be a requirement, and the Chapter 13 bankruptcies may become more the norm. You are wise to contact an attorney if you decide to file for bankruptcy.

CHAPTER 7 BANKRUPTCY

A Chapter 7, or straight bankruptcy, essentially asks the court to release you from all of your outstanding debt. Sound great? Think again. Before you can approach the court, you must sell off all of your assets to pay your creditors. Certain assets are excluded, such as your home; state laws vary. Be aware that some debts are not dissolved with a Chapter 7 filing. Taxes, student loans, alimony, and fines must still be paid.

To file, you need the appropriate forms. You can usually find these papers at a local stationery supply store or check online at www.allaboutforms.com. You'll also need information on the courthouse nearest you. You can check your telephone directory for the listing of the United States Bankruptcy Court.

Next, contact the bankruptcy clerk to find out what court you need to use based upon your district and county residency. Additionally ask the clerk what the time requirement is to qualify as a resident in that county before you can be eligible to file. There will be a filing fee when you turn in your forms at the courthouse.

On your filing day, you are no longer obligated to pay your outstanding debts. Notify your creditors immediately of your bankruptcy status, and provide them with the name and telephone number of your attorney. Follow up any verbal notification with a written letter. This should stop any collection efforts on their behalf.

CHAPTER 13 BANKRUPTCY

A Chapter 13 bankruptcy is different from a Chapter 7. With the new legislation, the Chapter 13 will be enforced more readily than the Chapter 7. Chapter 13 is essentially a federal repayment or wage earner's program. When you file, you work with the court to develop a budget that allows you to pay off your debts in whole or in part. The plan can take up to five years to complete. Once you're given a budget, you must learn to live on the terms established until your debt is paid off. The good news is, as long as you're under the court's supervision, you're protected from creditor harassment.

In many ways filing a Chapter 13 is fairly similar to working with a credit counseling and debt consolidation company. The downside is that the Chapter 13 is placed on your credit report as a public notice, which is viewed as a negative entry.

FILING

As with a Chapter 7, once you file your paperwork, you can notify creditors and collection agencies of your bankruptcy status; this will stop their efforts to contact you. If your wages are being garnished, you can stop this by immediately informing creditors of your bankruptcy filing. Be sure to do this in writing. A court-appointed trustee will be assigned to your Chapter 13 file, and he will then handle your payments, according to the terms set up.

Upon your completion of the program, the court forgives any remaining balances that you may have outstanding as long as they were covered in your plan. Your Chapter 13 bankruptcy will appear on your credit report. Each creditor listed on your repayment program will submit its own comments to the credit reporting agencies. This information may stay on your record up to ten years.

DIFFERENCES BETWEEN THE TWO TYPES OF BANKRUPTCY

A Chapter 7 bankruptcy clears most of your debt without you having to repay it. That's why it's called a straight bankruptcy. If your financial situation is such that you cannot possibly pay a significant portion of your debt within a realistic time frame, then you'll probably want to consider filing for a Chapter 7, but the court must approve it.

If it's possible for you to repay your debts over a given time, you may want to consider filing for a Chapter 13. Being under court supervision and protection may work for you. At least you'll have a plan of action in place. You'll also be able to hold on to any secured items you may have, such as cars, furniture, and so on, through making lower payments on them as outlined in your repayment plan.

COMPARING CHAPTER 13 WITH A DEBT MANAGEMENT COMPANY

Both Chapter 13 and a debt management company offer you repayment program options as a means to get out of debt. Both require you to make one monthly payment that they, in turn, pay to your creditors. The creditors may report to the credit reporting agencies. Both have their own fees; with a Chapter 13 you pay to file, and a debt management company usually assesses a monthly fee. You should be aware that future creditors view a Chapter 13 bankruptcy notice much more negatively than working with a debt management or credit counseling company.

If you miss a payment under a Chapter 13, you're protected from any creditor collection efforts. Under law, attempts to collect outstanding debt during a bankruptcy–court approved payment program are not allowed. On the other hand, if you're working with a debt management or credit counseling company and you miss a payment, no protection is offered.

With a Chapter 13 filing, you frequently repay less money than you actually owe. As I mentioned, if at the end of your repayment period you have remaining debt, these amounts are forgiven; you are not required to pay them. Your credit report, though, will reflect that payment was made to your creditors. Also, if you're facing a possible foreclosure on your home, a Chapter 13 can stop this action from being taken. Instead, you can have these payments extended over a five-year period or less.

By making payments through a debt management or credit counseling program, you will be paying off the full amounts of your debts. Most of the time the creditors pay the credit counseling and debt management companies a small percentage of the payment each month known as the "fair share."

Should you pay less than the amount agreed to under the terms of your repayment plan, a negative entry will be noted on your credit report. It will be recorded as a late payment.

Fully explore all of your options. Arrange an informative meeting with credit counselors and bankruptcy attorneys. The decision to declare bankruptcy should not be made without careful and thorough consideration.

CREDIT RESTORATION POST-BANKRUPTCY

If you've declared bankruptcy, it may seem that you'll never be able to qualify for new credit. Take heart. It is possible. You just need to understand the process, plan accordingly, and then rebuild your credit. For example, a bankruptcy is reflected on your credit report for up to ten years. However, you can attempt to rebuild your credit immediately.

How is this possible? Well, recall that creditors look for certain things: steady employment, long-term residency, payment habits, and your checking and savings accounts. They will examine these elements and how you've established and handled them after bankruptcy.

Before you begin to rebuild your credit, make sure that you have fully resolved your problems and that you have broken your old spending habits. It will take a lot of effort on your part to rebuild your credit, so if you feel you can't take on that project yet, don't. Overcoming the behavior that got you into financial distress can be the toughest element to face and rectify.

Reestablishing credit is similar to establishing credit for the first time. Refer back to Chapter 7.

DEBTORS ANONYMOUS

Sharing similarities with Alcoholics Anonymous, the Debtors Anonymous program offers support methods to attendees who are overspenders or who seek to gain control of their finances. You may wish to contact Debtors Anonymous and ask about their services. The group has offices across the nation.

AUTOMOBILES AND MORTGAGES

Automobile purchases and mortgages are great concerns for individuals who have filed for bankruptcy.

AUTOMOBILES

Look in your local listings for dealerships that specialize in selling automobiles to customers who have had bad credit or have been bankrupt. Frequently these dealers advertise in regional auto listing papers. Again, expect to put down a large deposit. The interest rates you'll be charged will be high as well.

The car you select to buy will be the collateral for your loan, which is why these dealers are willing to offer you special assistance. Make all your payments on time, and see to it that the company financing the car reports to the credit reporting agencies. This will help you reestablish a positive credit rating.

If you are paying a higher interest rate, after six months of making your payments on time, contact your bank or credit union about refinancing the car loan with a lower interest rate.

If you had a cosigner on the car loan, after making several payments on time, contact your bank or credit union to refinance the car in your name by removing the cosigner from the contract. This is better for you and your cosigner.

LETTIE'S STORY

Lettie called my office wanting help to get into a position to purchase a home. She had gone through a messy divorce, and her credit report was in bad shape. Accounts were on her report that belonged to her ex-husband; plus there was a bankruptcy.

After reviewing her credit report, I instructed Lettie to get two new lines of credit. She opened two secured credit card accounts and began making small purchases to establish a payment history on her credit report.

Several months later as her credit report began looking better, Lettie indicated that she had only two more car payments to make and her car would be paid off.

I went back to her credit report and discovered that there was no credit history about the car she was making payments on. Lettie had bought the car used three years prior with the main purpose of establishing credit in her name. She was paying a high interest rate, and the car was not dependable.

Lettie was devastated. I knew she needed a new car and referred her to a company that could help her get the new car and that reported payments to the credit reporting agencies.

Lettie went down to the car dealership and was able to purchase a new car with a low interest rate. She was thrilled. Not long after that, she was able to qualify for the home of her dreams.

MORTGAGES

Two years after your bankruptcy, you can try to qualify for a mortgage. A mortgage company will want to see that credit has been reestablished and that your accounts are in good standing.

If there is even one negative entry listed on your credit report since your bankruptcy, you will be denied. You should have a lender prequalify you for a loan prior to looking for that new home. Be honest about your past. With this information, the lender can try to secure the best possible loan for you. You may have to pay a higher interest rate, but do it! With property values rising, you can end up pricing yourself out of the market by waiting too long.

If you end up with a high interest rate, wait two years and then refinance to get a lower interest. By then you would have at least four years behind you since the bankruptcy and a good payment history.

WRAP-UP

Surviving any financial disaster is both tiring and distressing, but it can be done. If you've declared bankruptcy, know that it will take time and effort to rebuild your credit portfolio. Instead of focusing on the past, put your energy into the future.

Learn from your mistakes. Educate yourself about the best ways to reestablish yourself. Address old behavioral habits, and change the ones that caused you to wind up in serious financial straits. Then come up with a plan of attack, and implement it. Do not be afraid to seek outside advice from reputable sources. As long as you are patient and consistent with your efforts, you can become credit-worthy once again.

COACH'S TIP

The Web site for the Federal Trade Commission offers financial information of all kinds. The publications section provides information regarding bankruptcy that you can review or download at no cost. The address is www.ftc.gov.

14

TRIM THE FAT!

———

Debt places a heavy weight on your shoulders. Excessive debt causes stress, anxiety, and many sleepless nights.

It seems that everywhere you go, someone is trying to entice you to buy something. It can be hard to withstand the constant onslaught of messages urging you to spend, spend, spend. But withstand it you must. Advertisers and retailers want you to believe that you are what you buy. It's their business—and your pocketbook.

Yet the reality is, you're so much more than that. If you're ever going to get out of debt, you must change how you think about money, spending, and yourself. Rather than be anxious about your debt, concern yourself with it. That's right. Make reducing it a priority. Once you do so, your anxiety will diminish, perhaps not immediately, but sooner instead of later.

Get angry at the stores and businesses that are enticing you. Fight back! Don't let them win by causing you to pull out the plastic and spend. They are the ones benefiting from the finance charges and interest that you'll pay. The creditors' enticement is to find individuals who charge and keep a rolling balance on their credit cards so they can make money.

Not only that, the credit card company charges the creditor or merchant anytime you use your credit card as well as making money from you. The credit card company is smiling. It makes money on both ends. Get mad! Don't let it outsmart you. Pay cash!

COME UP WITH A PLAN

Now that reducing your debt is a primary goal in your life, you're ready to deal with the reality of your situation. You need to come up with a plan that will help you decrease the amount of current debt. Review your spending journal so you can see exactly where your money goes. After a month you'll know where to cut back.

WORKOUT

Get busy! Write down your plan of action in your journal. Carefully think about what you want to do, but don't pressure yourself to come up with the perfect plan. Expect to make some adjustments as you progress with your plan. Remember, action is the key to making your financial situation change.

Now let's see how much you really know about your debt. Your first exercise is to write down by memory (don't look at your statements) what you think each credit card balance is, the monthly minimum payment, the creditor name, and the interest. Total the amounts.

The second exercise is to look at your statements and list all of your credit cards and accounts on which you currently make monthly payments. Include the following: creditor's name, current balance, current minimum payment, interest rate, and credit limit.

Include medical bills, student loans, collection agencies, bank loans, and money you owe to *anyone*. Do you have any debts that you're not making payments on (even if you should be doing so)? Put them down.

Now here's the hard part. Total up everything. How did the second exercise's totals compare to the first exercise's totals? Was it a reality check for you?

YOLANDA'S STORY

Yolanda heard me on a radio talk show and called my office to get help. She indicated that she had $40,000 of debt that she wanted to consolidate with a home loan.

I took her loan application and had her credit report run. As I reviewed her credit report, I noticed there were too many pages with numerous accounts that appeared open. As I totaled the amount of outstanding debt, not including her mortgage, I discovered she was $100,000 in debt, not $40,000.

I dreaded making the telephone call to Yolanda, having to tell her the truth about her debt. After I broke the news to her, there was dead silence for what seemed an eternity. She quietly said, "I guess it got away from me. I had no idea."

There was nothing I could do to help her with the refinance or equity line for her home. The best advice I could give her was to refer her to a debt management company to help her consolidate her bills.

What about you? Are you living in the real world, or have things gotten away from you? Don't panic if this is a wake-up call. We're going to come up with a plan to get you out of this situation. Once you have a plan, you will gain control, and that will make you feel much better. We're going to focus on reducing your credit debt first.

If you have an account or debt that you're not currently making payments on, leave that information blank for now.

You must stop using your credit cards. In order for this plan to work (i.e., reduce your credit debt), you mustn't incur any more new debt. If you need to take the cards out of your wallet and put them into a safe place, do so. Freeze the credit cards in a block of ice, or put them in a safe deposit box at the bank. Whatever you need to do to stop you from using your credit cards, do it!

From here on in, you'll use only cash to make your purchases. When you're shopping, think twice and hard about a purchase. You'll be surprised at how you reduce your spending when you rely only on cash.

If you like the feel of plastic, use your ATM or debit card. It's the same as cash. But don't forget to enter the purchase in your check registry to deduct from your checking or savings balance.

TRANSFERRING CARD BALANCES

Let's go back to your list for a moment. Do you have any major credit cards that are not delinquent or maxed out? What are the interest rates on these cards? Is it possible for you to transfer your high-interest credit card balances to cards with a lower interest rate? If you can, do it.

Then take the higher-interest-rate cards and cut them up. Mail these cards to the creditors, including instructions to close your account. Send everything via certified mail with a return receipt. Keep copies of your correspondence for your files.

You will apply the payment that you would have been making to these companies to the lower-interest-rate cards. For example, if you were paying $150 per month on the credit card you transferred, add the $150 to the lower-interest credit card monthly payment. Doing this will help you decrease your balance much more quickly and save you interest charges.

CREDIT CARD PAY-OFF STRATEGY

After you have reviewed your debt list, prioritize each credit card from the highest credit card balance to the lowest credit card balance, for example:

Abbott Company	$2,400
Lyons Company	$1,500
Beta Credit Card	$1,000
Department Store	$500
Department Store	$275

Experts have different opinions about which to pay off first: high interest with high balances or high interest with low balances. The decision is yours, but the quickest way to get out of debt and feel that you are accomplishing something is to pay off the lower balances first. The payment you would be making to the lowest balance, now that it's paid off, should be added to the next credit card balance you are trying to pay off. For instance, the balance of $275 had a payment of $15. Once you pay this off, add the $15 to the minimum payment to the next balance of $500 and continue doing this until it is paid off. Then take the two payments you were making on the department store account, and add the amount to the next credit card balance in addition to the minimum payment. These extra payments will apply to the principal and cause the balances to decrease rapidly.

CALCULATE YOUR YEARLY ESTIMATED PAYMENTS

At the beginning of each year add up an estimated amount to be paid toward credit card debt, and divide that amount by twelve (months). As your balances decrease, your minimum payments will decrease. Use the amount that you estimated to continue paying the balances down. Don't gauge it by the minimum amount on your statement.

For example, if you have calculated that $6,000 per year will be paid toward credit card debt, you divide that by twelve months. This equals $500 per month toward credit card bills. Since the balances are decreasing and the minimum payments are being reduced, you need to stay with your plan while continuing to budget $500 per month and apply the excess to whatever credit card you want to pay off first. Don't look at excess money as extra until your debts are paid off.

INCREASING YOUR MONTHLY PAYMENT

Another thing you can do to reduce your credit card debt is to make extra payments on your accounts. When you make the minimum payment, you're simply stretching out the debt and making more money for the creditor. Here's an example. You have a balance of $2,000, and you've just stopped making charges on that card. It will take you more than sixteen years to pay back this amount with minimum monthly payments. You'll also be paying approximately $2,504.62 in interest charges. That is why I strongly urge you to pay off that debt as soon as possible rather than stretch it out by making only the minimum payment. Think about this. If you tagged on an extra $5 to your monthly payment, you'd shave six years off that sixteen-year time frame as well as save interest charges of $738.59. Boost that extra monthly amount up by $10, and you lose eight years and save interest of $1,113.70. So you see, with just a little bit of strategizing, it truly is possible to reduce your credit debt.

Remember when you pay off the balance of one account, take

the money you previously allocated to that debt, and apply it to another payment. Doing this will shorten the time it takes to pay off your current debt. Continue to use this trick on all of your outstanding accounts until you're all paid off. Stay out of credit card debt by taking the money that you would have used to pay your old accounts and pay yourself instead. Put that money into a savings account so you'll have something for your future.

REFINANCING, OR HOME EQUITY LOANS

If you're a homeowner, you might consider refinancing your home to reduce your monthly debt. If you don't want to refinance your home, but want to get cash to consolidate your bills, you could get a home equity loan or a second mortgage. Here are a few things to think about:

- How much will you actually save each month?

- How long do you intend to live in your home?

- Are you willing to extend the terms of your debt load?

When you refinance your first mortgage to get cash out, you must have enough equity in your property to be approved by a lender. Generally this is 75 to 80 percent of the property appraisal value minus the amount still owed on it. An equity loan or second mortgage will loan up to 100 percent of the appraised value minus the balance owed on the first mortgage

Refinancing could be a smart move for you if you're presently paying one percentage point (at least) above the going rate. Keep in mind that you want to balance any reductions in payments with the overall cost of the loan. If you want to consolidate bills, your monthly mortgage rate needs to be less than the total of your bills and mortgage combined. If you are paying $500 in monthly credit payments and your monthly mortgage cost is $1,000, you're paying a combined total of $1,500. If you calculate the refinancing numbers and they are lower than $1,500—say $1,200—then you're saving $300 a month. Your savings could then be applied to any outstanding credit debt, accelerating your ability to bring down those balances or putting your savings into an interest-bearing account for your future.

If you decide to refinance, make sure your payments are reduced. If this isn't the case, don't refinance. You don't want to increase your debt or payments if you're already having problems making ends meet. You'll also want to be comfortable with the idea of extending the terms of your mortgage. By refinancing or taking out a new second mortgage, you've increased the number of years it will take you to pay off the mortgage.

If you refinance or take out a second mortgage, will you be able to pay off all of your debts or at least the majority of your debts, not including the mortgage? If your answer is yes, go ahead and consider refinancing or getting a second mortgage.

You will have loan fees, and the new mortgage may take fifteen to thirty years to pay off. You should live in your home at least 12 to 18 months after you take out the loan to recoup your closing costs since the majority of the time the closing costs are added into the loan. If your debts will be paid off within five years, don't re-finance or get a new second mortgage.

Several Web sites offer easy and convenient resources that can help you determine whether refinancing is right for you:

- www.bankrate.com. In addition to online calculators to help you crunch the numbers, this site explains refinancing, offering several scenarios.

- www.hsh.com. You can search this site for mortgage rates by state. If you're interested in shopping around for the best mortgage deal, order the mortgage shopping kit. The site also offers free calculators.

- www.homestore.com. This site has a handy refinancing guide for you to peruse. It also features a user-friendly calculator.

- www.iown.com. You've decided to refinance. Visit this site to get help with figuring out your goals and how to accomplish them.

Use these sites as references. Don't fill out a loan application online giving your name, address, Social Security number, and so on. Remember, excessive inquiries hurt your credit score. Contact a local mortgage broker and check whether its rates are competitive.

MORTGAGE REDUCTION PLAN

If you'd like to decrease the number of years you have to pay on your mortgage, you can set yourself up on a mortgage reduction plan. Essentially you increase the amount of your monthly house payment.

Just by adding one extra payment per year, you can reduce the life of your mortgage by nearly half. For example, if your mortgage has a life of thirty years (typical term), it's possible that you could shorten that time to fifteen or seventeen years. This could potentially save you hundreds of thousands of dollars. If you add more money to your payment than required, indicate that you want to apply it to the principal. Check your note on your mortgage to see if you have a prepayment penalty.

Try visiting one of the Web sites listed to run the numbers and see how you could cut your costs.

REFINANCING YOUR CAR

In most cases you can lower your monthly payment by refinancing your car. Basically a bank or lender takes the blue book value of your car and subtracts the amount that you owe. The blue book value is a standard price list that is commonly used to determine the value of an automobile. Using the difference between your loan amount and the amount that you currently owe, the bank or lender gives you cash based on that difference.

Here's an example. The blue book value is $8,000 for your car. You still have $4,000 to pay on it. The equity or cash that you'd receive from refinancing your car would be $4,000. You could then use this money to eliminate other outstanding debt. Once that is paid off, you can make higher monthly payments on your car to shorten the time of that loan. You'll want to print directions on your payment coupon, something like "The difference of this payment is to be applied to my principal."

MAJOR ASSETS

Do you happen to have any items that you can live without, for instance, jewelry, electronic equipment, a computer, furniture, a car, or even a home? You can sell such items, especially if they have a good resale value, to raise cash to pay off outstanding debt.

On an item with a loan, such as a home or vehicle, you can sell the item and use the money to pay off the loan. Obviously if you sold your home, the money gained could be significant. Calculate the numbers first, though. Let's say you bought your home for

$300,000. Your first mortgage was for $220,000, and you had a second mortgage on the property for $30,000. The amount you'd make—minus closing costs of approximately $18,000—would be $32,000. You could use this money to pay off outstanding debt and apply the remainder to a new home.

You may have assets that you can sell outright because you don't owe any money on them. You wouldn't want to sell great-grandma's heirloom necklace if it has a great deal of sentimental value to you and your family. But if you happen to own artwork, antiques, fine jewelry, electronic equipment, or anything else that you don't use or could live without, sell it.

Then apply the amount gained to your outstanding debt.

WORKOUT

LIST YOUR ASSETS

List your assets that you could sell to raise cash. Include unwanted or unused furniture, jewelry, electronic equipment, cars, motorcycles, exercise and sports equipment, anything you own that has substantial value.

PAYDAY LOAN COMPANIES

Perhaps you've heard about payday loan companies. These companies offer a short-term deferred deposit loan. In other words they offer you money against your paycheck.

People who have bad credit are often tempted to take out a payday loan when they run short of cash. The reason is that these companies require only two things: a regular paycheck and a basic checking account. Payday companies then charge them $15 to $30 in exchange for loaning the money. This is an extremely high rate.

Payday loan companies haven't been around long enough for their business to be regulated. Most financial experts will tell you to avoid a payday loan company altogether.

PAWNSHOPS

Oftentimes, people think of pawnshops when they're trying to raise quick cash. If you want to keep the item you intend to pawn, I don't recommend pawning it unless you're really in a desperate situation. Why? When you pawn something—antiques, a camera, electronic equipment, jewelry, a musical instrument, and the like—a pawnbroker gives you a loan on the item in exchange for keeping it. Pawnbrokers offer only 50 to 60 percent of an item's resale value.

TAX REFUNDS

Each year a number of us receive a tax refund and think of it as bonus money. But now that you're focusing on reducing your debt, the smart thing to do would be to take that money and pay off some of your debt or put money into savings.

You may also want to think about how your return was prepared. If the IRS owed you a significant sum of money, those dollars could be working for you—be it in extra payments on current outstanding credit accounts or in an interest-generating bank account.

If your employer is withholding too much money, consider increasing your number of dependents so that you can receive the excess money with each paycheck rather than once a year with a tax refund. Why should Uncle Sam earn interest on your money? Make your money work for you.

A PART-TIME JOB

You can create additional income through a part-time job if you need help handling your present debt load. Calculate whether the amount of money you'll make is worth the time and extra effort you'll put into this second position. Consider such factors as the time to travel to and from the second job, the cost of travel, and food expenses. If you take on a part-time job, will you need to pay for additional things, such as childcare and clothing? If these costs add up, significantly detracting from your ability to pay off your bills, then it's not really worthwhile for you to take on another job.

You may try to put in overtime hours at your present position. You may think about asking for a raise if you're in the position to do so. You may ask around for small part-time work. Sometimes friends and neighbors will pay you to do simple chores, such as gardening, house-sitting, baby-sitting, or housework, on an occasional basis.

MONEY-MAKING HOBBIES

If you have a hobby that you enjoy doing, you may be able to make some money from it. Each of us is born with God-given gifts and talents. Are you good at any of the following: crafts, electronic repair, painting, typing, cooking, photography, writing, illustrating, sewing? People are always in need of these services.

Think about how you could advertise your skills and generate extra income by picking up some part-time work. You may have skills that you don't employ to make money. The nice thing about making money this way is that you're doing something that you enjoy, which can boost your spirits when working those extra hours. Plus, you'll be helping others, which will make you feel good too.

Susan enjoyed cooking. When she found herself getting in debt, she decided to use her cooking skills to make money. Susan had several friends who worked outside the home and dreaded preparing meals when they came home from work. She offered to cook them meals and charge them for doing it. Needless to say, the idea was a success. Susan was able to make money doing what she liked as well as make her friends happy and well-fed.

THE BARTER SYSTEM

True, it's old-fashioned to barter for goods and services. However, it is a way to obtain the things you need without incurring more debt. If you can trade a skill, service, or item for something in return, I strongly suggest this approach. More often than not, the most difficult thing about bartering is making the offer. You'll never know if you don't ask, and frequently you'll be pleasantly surprised by the answer.

You can swap items such as clothing, accessories, household goods, or books that you've grown tired of with friends. Set a date when everyone can get together. You'll need some space to display the items, then negotiate your trades. This is a great way to get rid of items that have been sitting around, and you get "new" stuff without spending any money. This system is very handy, especially if you have children. You can pass on clothes they've outgrown to someone whose kids can still use them.

You can take this thrifty approach one step farther by throwing a potluck. That way you can provide inexpensive refreshments as well as gloat over your new items.

When my middle daughter, Christy, prepared for her wedding, she was having a hard time finding perfect bridesmaids dresses. I knew a woman who was a seamstress and talked to her about this. As it turned out, this woman needed help with her credit and finances, so we bartered. She designed and made the bridesmaids' dresses in exchange for my service. It was a great exchange, and the wedding was beautiful.

FAMILY AND FRIENDS

This option can be a sensitive one. Is it possible for you to take out a loan from a family member or a friend? Before you approach her or him, make sure that the money loaned won't be missed or undermine that person's own financial security. Have a plan before you talk to them.

Explain that you're working on reducing your debt and that you've developed a plan that requires obtaining a lump sum. Let them know how you intend to repay them and the length of time involved; be realistic, and be responsible. You may even want to offer interest, but make sure the amount is lower than what a bank would charge. The point is to make them feel safe about loaning you money, and not for you to incur more debt.

If you can't repay the loan in a timely fashion, you may want to reconsider making the proposal. Money matters can create some heated arguments. If you're experiencing financial difficulties, inform your relative or friend of your circumstances. He or she should be able to be flexible about the loan payments, and if they aren't, it's probably not a good idea to take his money.

DEBT MANAGEMENT COMPANY

You should consider contacting a credit counseling company to consolidate your debt, whether you are delinquent in your payments, are overextended with your credit cards, or are tired of paying high interest rates.

Credit counselors become the middle party in communicating with your creditors. They will help you work out your problems and develop a repayment program between you and your creditors.

Most debt consolidation companies offer a nonprofit service. A small monthly donation and small percentage (called the fair share) are paid to the company from the creditor.

When you contact a credit counselor, have a list of your bills ready and information regarding your income and living expenses available. The counselor will look at your income, assets, debt, and expenses to determine what you can afford to pay. The counselor needs to see the whole picture to develop a payment plan that will help you and satisfy the creditors.

Once the counselor receives all the required information from you regarding your financial situation, he contacts your creditors to work out a repayment schedule. The credit counselor will work with each creditor to lower the payment by reducing the interest as low as zero to eleven percent. Each creditor will use a different formula to lower the rate.

By reducing your interest rate, the payments that you will be making will drop below what you are paying now. The payments will apply more toward your principal, which will allow you to pay off your debts in four to six years. You will save thousands of dollars in interest and be debt free. Your late fees and over-the-limit fees will stop being accrued by working with a credit counseling company. If you are late, the account will be re-aged and brought current.

The credit counseling company will set your payments so that you are paying one monthly payment to the counseling service to cover all your debts. The counseling service will then disburse the payments to the creditors. You will know every month how much you will be spending toward your bills.

WRAP-UP

It may seem that it will take forever until you've paid off all of your debt. With your plan in hand, you should be able to get a good sense of how long that "forever" truly is. Consistently review your plan. Take comfort in seeing your progress. After all, ignoring your bills will not make them go away. Focus instead on how you no longer have to worry about bills that you've already paid off. Think about how you've managed to take control of your spending.

While you're at it, dream up some other financial goals that you want to achieve. The same tactics you used to reduce your debt can be applied to accomplishing other tasks too. By managing your money wisely, you can create financial opportunity and security.

COACH'S TIP

In your battle against debt, keep in mind my general rule of thumb: if you can't pay cash for it, then you probably can't afford it.

15

Controlling Yourself: The B Word

In this chapter the B word is not a bad word, but I did get your attention. My B word is a good word—it can help you change your life. You may kick, scream, and cry that you can't do it, but *budgeting* is the key to your financial success, which will ultimately bring you security and peace of mind.

Too many women live in the financial here and now. That is, they rarely put money into savings, they live primarily and precariously from paycheck to paycheck, and they feel it's more important to look as if they have money than it is to really have it. A new pair of designer shoes, or money for your savings account? Studies show that a lot of us opt for the shoes. Quite frankly this isn't the road to financial security; it's more like the road to financial obscurity.

CHANGING YOUR WAYS

Putting yourself on the right path isn't tremendously difficult. It may require you to change your outlook and your thinking about money and spending, and it may cause you some initial frustration as you change your behavior patterns. But you most definitely can do it. And to do it, you need to come up with a budget and then stick with it. It's all up to you.

A budget is simply a tool to show you where your cash goes. Rather than reacting to your expenses and bills as they come in, a budget helps you allocate money for anticipated costs, for special things, such as trips or those expensive shoes or purse, and for savings. With a plan, it is easier to make adjustments and see where you may be wasting your cash.

WRITE IT DOWN

One of the most important steps in building your budget and gaining control over your finances is to calculate your net worth. If you applied for a business loan, a home loan, or an automobile loan, you would complete an application that would give the potential lender an idea of your net worth. You calculate your net worth by identifying your total assets and subtracting your total liabilities. You should calculate your net worth at the beginning of every year to see your progress in accomplishing your goals.

SETTING UP YOUR BUDGET

Setting up a budget and sticking to it is time consuming and at times stressful. A budget takes discipline and accountability, but the benefits are rewarding. The goals you want to accomplish will happen much more quickly if you write them down on paper.

To come up with your budget, write down all the debts and payments you are making. Include everything—your living expenses too. Then make a list of the money you have coming in monthly.

You need to know exactly what you owe, what your payments are, and what income you have on a monthly basis.

If you are having trouble doing this, you can look at living expenses from the past year to calculate your general household costs. Review check registers and credit card statements for the amounts you spent over the past year for things like rent/mortgage, food, utilities, transportation, childcare, insurance, and medical expenses.

You can list all of your expenses on a piece of paper. Or you may want to use a computer software program or try an online Web site to come up with your budget. Whatever system you use, list everything you owe.

SELF-EMPLOYMENT

If you're self-employed or have income based on commissions, refer to your previous year's expense totals. Tally up your costs, and then divide by twelve to see how much money you need per month to live on. This will be your average for monthly expenditures. If you make more income in some months than other months, do not spend that money freely. Instead, stick to your monthly budget, and put the rest aside in savings. Strive to stay three to six months ahead of your budget. That way, when the leaner months hit, you'll have money to cover your expenditures. It will also help you escape the living-from-month-to-month scenario.

THE BUDGET BUSTERS

Expenditures that may have to be paid yearly, quarterly, or monthly must be added to your monthly budget.

Separate your monthly and yearly expenses into two categories.

The budget busters (nonmonthly expenses) will fall into your yearly expenditures, because most people forget to set aside money to pay these items. Examples include property taxes, home insurance, and car maintenance. Suppose your property tax bill is $1,200 per year. Divide the bill by twelve (number of months in year). This equals $100. Set aside $100 each month so you can pay when it's due.

The items in the budget buster categories should force you to save for these expenses so you will not be short when the bills come due. Open a separate savings account so you aren't tempted to spend it.

NONMONTHLY EXPENSES OR BUDGET BUSTERS

Property taxes

Home insurance

Security systems

Home repairs/maintenance (yard)

Maintenance agreements

Waste management

Auto registrations (all vehicles)

Life insurance

Disability insurance

Doctor/dental

Orthodontia

Vision exam/contacts/glasses

Health maintenance

Church tithing

Organizations/clubs

Professional licenses

Sports

Warehouse clubs

Books/supplies

Work clothing

Office equipment maintenance

Water/water softener

Association fees

Club memberships

Automobile insurance

Auto maintenance and repairs

Medical insurance

Sports clothes

Recreational hobbies

Vacations

Music lessons

Pet maintenance

Accountant

Taxes

Savings

Investments

Holidays

Others

School tuition

Magazines

School uniforms

Clothes (adult and children)

Gifts (birthday, anniversary, etc.)

Again if you're not sure what you spend, refer to your check registry and past credit card statements for the last twelve months.

Determine what items you must pay throughout the year. In your journal list each item, the amount, and the month due.

With the amounts totaled, divide by twelve (months). This equals the amount each month that you must set aside. It also is the total to enter on your Personal Monthly Budget Workout.

BUDGET RESULTS

How did you fare with your budget? Did you have excess money after your budget was set up, or did you have a shortage?

Now compare your money paid out total with your money paid in total. Do you have enough money to cover the basic costs of your lifestyle? If you're overspending, don't panic because the following chapters will show you ways to save money and methods to get out of debt to free your money for savings.

Experts say you should have at least $1,000 saved in an emergency fund—not credit cards, but a safe account that earns you interest. If $1,000 seems too much for you right now, then start somewhere. Something is always better than nothing. If you can start with $100, then do that. Add to that account on a monthly basis.

Having three to six months of living expenses set aside in case of emergency will bring you peace of mind. If you have a single-family income, save six months of living expenses. If your husband and you work, then three months' reserve is the goal.

The following is a recommendation of the percentage amounts that should go into each category of your budget:

- Housing—35 percent of your income
- Debt—15 percent of your income

- Travel—15 percent of your income
- Other—25 percent of your income (tithing and charitable giving should be included in this category)
- Savings—10 percent of your income

ANALYZING YOUR BUDGET

Whether you have extra money left over or no money at all, it's a good idea to analyze your budget. You may be able to make some cuts in one category that will allow you to pay off outstanding debt, set aside money for savings, or invest in your retirement. The beauty of a budget is that it enables you to get an overall financial picture, and then decide where you want or need your money to go. You control its flow; the flow doesn't control you.

CHECK IN

If some of these numbers are causing your head to spin, sit back and give yourself some time to adjust to these new perspectives. Maybe the clear picture you suddenly have of your finances shocks you. Remind yourself that budgeting is not meant to force you into an overly ascetic, deprived, joyless lifestyle. A budget empowers you by letting you know how much income comes in, how much goes out, and how much you can save for yourself and your future needs. Your goal is to live within your means. Focus on how good you'll feel when you know your expenses are covered.

WRAP-UP

When you get your finances under control, you can begin to save money. Instead of spending more, your new mind-set should be saving more. Knowing you have money to cover your costs with some set aside for emergencies will allow you to enjoy your life more abundantly. You won't constantly be worrying about making ends meet. Likewise, building genuine financial security, be it money in the bank for your children's college tuition or your future retirement, will increase your sense of well-being. Even if you're saving money for a major appliance or a long-term goal, you'll feel the confidence of managing your money and making it work for you.

Ultimately, by working with your budget, you'll see exactly where you want to put your precious dollars and how you can make them work for you. Once you're free of outstanding debt, reserve your credit card for major purchases, and plan ahead so that you can pay off as much of that type of debt as possible.

Keep your costs low so that you can increase your savings. Think about what you want your money to do, and review your short- and long-term financial goals. You may want to consult a financial adviser to help you set up multiple goals, such as home ownership, savings for yourself and your children, investments, and retirement.

COACH'S TIP

If you have setbacks along the way, revisit your plan and adjust it. Don't give up. After time has passed, you will see a difference, and you will be steps closer to your dream of financial security.

16

Tips for Saving Money

———

Y ou've just worked your way through crafting a budget. In the process, you may have collapsed on the floor due to sheer mental exhaustion. Getting the numbers to work for you can be a real challenge. Well, pick yourself up, and get ready for some handy money-saving tips. Maybe your budget numbers could use an infusion of extra cash, or perhaps you want to set aside some dollars for savings, retirement, a vacation, your child's college education, a car, or a home. Whatever your goal, some of the tips in this chapter are sure to help you pinch a few extra pennies.

BUT FIRST, HAVE YOU PAID DOWN YOUR DEBT?

I know you may groan when you read that question. But I cannot overemphasize how important it is for you to rid yourself of debt. If you're seeking financial security, the debt has to go. And don't think I don't know how much debt you are carrying.

On average, the American household possesses five or six credit cards. The average combined debt owed on all of these cards totals

$15,000 to $20,000. It's no wonder Americans have a hard time saving. We're too busy spending (and charging what we buy).

So put away those credit cards, and pay that debt down! Spend within your means, and use some of these tips to help you in your debt crusade. When you've taken care of the debt, keep using the tips to help you save extra cash.

TOM AND NICOLE'S STORY

For years Tom and Nicole had been consistently using their credit cards. With small monthly minimums, it didn't really seem to be a big deal at first. But then bill problems set in. They turned to their families to bail them out. But without curbing their credit card habits, things seemed to get worse and worse for the couple. They appreciated the help their families gave them but felt ashamed and guilty always asking for money to pay their costs. Each month it was the same—not enough money to make ends meet or pay off anybody from whom they'd borrowed money.

Both wondered whether it was time to throw in the towel and declare bankruptcy. Still, that seemed a desperate measure. They continued to hope that someday they could get their finances under control and pay off their creditors and their families.

That's when they made an appointment with me. I instructed Tom and Nicole to make a list of all their outstanding bills, the amount of their income, and their living expenses. Judging from the lists, there really shouldn't have been a problem. Clearly things weren't adding up.

So I asked the couple about their miscellaneous spending. Did they eat out frequently? What about shopping for clothes and entertainment items? They looked at me. Neither one had any idea how much money was going toward such costs. But yes, they did spend money on those things. We'd found the source of their overspending.

We needed to figure out how to break the habit of careless inciden-tal spending.

I told Tom and Nicole to purchase daily expense notepads. For the next thirty days, they were to write down each item, along with the amount spent. No expense was too small to be included.

After thirty days had passed, the couple returned to my office. We took their notes and broke them down into categories. Doing that allowed us to see where their incidental spending was adding up. Knowing that would help us control how they were spending money. Well, it turned out that Tom and Nicole ate out a lot, and they had a pricey coffeehouse habit. Just by cutting back on these two things, they were able to save nearly $200 a month. They were shocked that all those little things added up to so much. Using the money saved from lowering these costs, they were able to begin paying down their outstanding debt.

TRACK STARS

Often, people think that tracking their expenses, especially the small, day-to-day costs, is a waste of time. It's too hard to carry a notepad around and jot down every dime and dollar! Besides, how can some loose change and a couple of dollars here and there make a difference anyway?

Part of the reason I ask clients to track their expenses is to show them how all those seemingly small costs really add up. You may have already tracked your expenses when you prioritized your bills. But tracking where your cash goes is so important that we're doing it again. So you may want to review your expense journals and check your progress. Or you may need to bite the bullet and surrender to the fact that until you track your cash flow, you're not being honest with yourself, and you don't have a true picture of your financial condition.

Once you know where the money goes, you'll know exactly where you can cut back and make spending adjustments.

When you keep your expense log, jot down the details. Don't just pass the cost off as a miscellaneous item. Describe what it is, the date, and how much you spent. If you like, write in your journal about how you were feeling when you bought the item. Sometimes there are emotional attachments associated with miscellaneous purchases.

ATM WITHDRAWALS

There are two ways to approach your ATM withdrawals. One way is to withdraw only from ATM machines that don't charge you a fee. If you visit machines that are not affiliated with your bank, you can pay $4 or more in fees on just one transaction. Do this five times in one month, and that adds up to $20.

The second approach is to budget your daily cash expenses in advance and take out only that amount each week. Then try to stick to that weekly cash amount. Otherwise, every time you take out money from the ATM, write it down in your notepad. Don't take out $20 and fail to account for how you spent it. List each penny of that withdrawal.

Most people have no idea what they spend these withdrawals on, even though they'll note the transaction in their check ledger. Don't make the mistake of spending what you have in your account each month until it's gone. Exercise control over your money and spending.

CASH AND CREDIT CARD JOURNALS

Make a list of purchase categories—dining out, fast food, clothing, coffee, gasoline, magazines, CDs, movies, prescriptions, and personal toiletries—in your journal or notepad. List what you spend in each applicable category. After thirty days total each category. Add up all the categories for a grand total. Surprised? Write about it in your journal.

The drill is essentially the same as the one you did for cash. Every time you use a credit card, write it down. Get in the habit of saving your receipts and comparing them with your monthly credit card statement too.

WHAT DID YOU DISCOVER ABOUT YOUR SPENDING HABITS?

After thirty days did you have any realizations about where your money goes? Are there ways to cut back on your spending so that you can save some money either for debt or for savings? Most experts will tell you that just about anyone can find a way to save 10 to 20 percent by examining daily cash and credit expenditures and making some adjustments.

OTHER WAYS TO CUT BACK

Many of us are lazy about checking our banking statements. However, it may pay to review your statements and see just how much you're paying for services. Could you get a better deal with another bank? Don't forget those additional ATM fees that you can avoid. Do you incur any merchant fees when you use your debit card with certain establishments? Well, then, there's another place you can cut back on service fees. Can you get a bank credit by using automatic deposit? Try to think of all the little ways you could save a few dollars here and there. Then add up those savings on a yearly projection. An extra $20 to $25 a month could be applied to high credit debt, which would help you bring those balances down faster and save you interest charges.

SAVE ON SODA

If you drink soda every day and buy it from a vending machine or a convenience store, you're probably paying about 60¢ per can. Did you know that if you brought that same soda from home, you'd be paying only about 25¢ per can? That's a considerable savings. Add up those savings on a monthly basis, and that's $7. Over the course of a year, you've saved nearly $90. And that's for only one soda. If you drink more than that each day, the savings are even greater. You can also cash in on recycled cans.

SPARE CHANGE

You know all that spare change you carry around in your purse or pockets? Or maybe you have it tossed here and there, stashed in different places around your home, car, or office. Change how you think about those extra coins. Gather up all your spare change, and put it into a container—a piggybank, a jar, anything will do. Think of this container as your savings. At the end of the month, take that money to the bank and deposit it into your savings. You'll be surprised at how it can add up.

DINING OUT

If you like to eat out, think twice before you do so. Avoid the added expense of dining out or even ordering takeout. Take the money you'd save and put it in a jar or piggybank. At the end of the month, add up your savings so you can see exactly how much money you would have spent, and then put it toward a bill or deposit it in the bank.

SHOPPING

Avoid unnecessary shopping. When you do go out, think carefully about your purchases. Is it something you really need? Keep a list of things you need, and then watch for sales. If you come across something especially tempting, go home and wait a day or two.

CUTTING BACK ON HOUSEHOLD COSTS

If yours is like many homes, you probably have cable services. Is it possible for you to cut back on any of these services? Maybe you can use the basic package for a few months just to keep costs down.

Review your phone bills, especially your long-distance costs. Then check out the various deals being advertised. You can save some money each month on lower bills, even if it's a few pennies here and there. At the end of the year, that money can add up.

What about additional costs such as call waiting, caller ID, and three-way calling? Do you have extra lines that you could do without?

If you belong to a health club or gym, examine what it costs you to have that membership. Is it possible for you to work out at home? You can work out with a number of excellent videos in your home, and you can use inexpensive workout tools. Resistance bands and dumbbells enable you to strength train, but you can also use homemade items such as cinder blocks for an aerobic step and weights made from canned vegetables or plastic bottles filled with sand. Or go for a brisk walk, ride your bike, or visit a local park for a friendly game of hoops. It can be quite pleasant to be outdoors instead of inside a gym—plus you get the benefits of working out.

When was the last time you reviewed the cost of your auto insurance policy? Different companies are anxious to get your business, so shop around for competitive prices. It's fairly easy to do this sort of thing online too.

Look over your medical care coverage. Can you save money by paying a higher deductible?

Garage sales and discount stores can offer you decent prices on clothes and toys. Secondhand stores are other money-saving options.

You can cut back on entertainment costs by renting movies rather than going to the movie theater. If you want to see a new release, opt for a matinee for cheaper ticket prices.

Cancel subscriptions to magazines and newspapers, and get your information from the television and radio.

Avoid buying lottery tickets and other sweepstakes contests in hopes of winning the "big one." It's nice to dream, but your chances of winning are pretty slim.

Save money on interest by paying off your credit card debt each month. Just by avoiding fees and carried-over balances, you'll save some cash.

WORKOUT

Tracking Your Extra Cash

Keep a list of the money you've saved over the past thirty days. Allow yourself to feel good about your new habits. Then make a list of all the things you can do with that saved money, such as pay down bills or grow your savings. Think of something you'd like to save for, and then put your money toward that goal. Enjoy the fruits of your penny-pinching efforts.

WRAP-UP

When you get into the habit of saving, it's easy to change your perspectives about spending. Allow yourself some treats every now and then, unless your finances are in really bad shape just track how much money you're allowing yourself to spend on such things. That's where most people trip themselves up. They have this little thought in the back of their minds that says again and again, *Well, that's not much.* Too much of this autopilot spending gets you into trouble.

Use your worksheets in your notepad or journal, and compare them at the end of thirty days. If you need to, repeat this exercise for another thirty days to help you ingrain your new spending and saving habits.

COACH'S TIP

I have a friend who started saving her money about two years ago. She's a writer, and having enough money to pay the bills has been a struggle for her. For years she thought that saving a few dollars here and there wouldn't add up. I ran into her, and she was so excited. She told me how wrong she'd been to think that. Once she started saving, she witnessed how the money grew. No wonder she was smiling.

Saving money takes practice. So don't think about it: do it. One day you'll be smiling too.

17

PROTECT YOURSELF:
COMMUNICATE!

———

One of the phrases you've heard me repeat frequently is, "Knowledge is empowerment." This is especially true when you're a woman dealing with finances. Knowing what your resources are, knowing how to manage them, and knowing how to save for your future should be fundamental aspects of your life.

Do not rely on someone else to take care of these things for you. When you do so, you become vulnerable to financial insecurity. Don't believe me?

- 33 percent to 66 percent of women between the ages of 35 and 55 will be living below the poverty line by age 70.

- 75 percent of women who marry will eventually be widowed

So, even if you do marry, there will be times when it's up to you to manage the money. Clearly it just makes good sense to be knowledgeable about your finances. But there's one other tool you'll need, and that's communication.

Communication takes time and effort. It involves asking questions and being able to explain your own personal concerns. It means taking you and your own needs seriously. It's not unusual for women to put aside their own needs for the sake of others. Taking care of yourself, however, is not an extra—it's a necessity, whether you're single, married, or divorced. So don't be afraid to speak up for yourself.

SINGLE LADIES

Single women have to take care of themselves. They're in charge of their own finances—which can be a wonderful thing. Have no fears about educating yourself as early as possible about financial management. Don't put things off for another day. Make a point to start saving money for your future right now, even if that means stashing a few crumpled dollars in a mason jar each week. The point is to build financial security, and the only way that'll happen is if you take small steps consistently.

In addition to this book, there are numerous financial resources for you to take advantage of. Pick an area of your life, such as budgeting, savings, or investments, that you want to gain control of, and focus your efforts on it. When you feel confident with what you've learned, move onto another topic. You can check out financial books and magazines from your local public library. Bookstores offer many different kinds of personal finance materials as well. There are even online sites dedicated to women and finance. Find one that suits your needs:

- Women's Financial Network

- Financialmuse.com

- MsMoney.com
- WomenCONNECT.com
- Ka-Ching
- ivillage.com
- Women.com

And don't be afraid to get advice and opinions from people you trust. Most importantly, always protect yourself and your financial credibility. To illustrate what I mean, let's take a look at one woman's story.

Lucy's Story

Lucy was a bright, articulate, successful young woman. We met because she had a credit problem. Lucy had an ex-boyfriend who'd ruined her credit. Back when they were dating, she had opened up three credit card accounts for him. He told her that he'd had credit issues in the past. She was in love, and she wanted to help him out, so she opened up the credit card accounts using her name.

At first he was good about making the payments. Lucy was proud of him. But when she went away on a business trip, he started charging again and was soon maxed out on all of the cards. Well, the relationship ended shortly thereafter, too. Except that Lucy was now saddled with collectors coming after her for the money owed. Her own credit was ruined. To make matters worse, her ex-boyfriend filed for bankruptcy, which also reflected on her accounts.

Since then, Lucy married, and she and her husband wanted to buy a home. Her husband was aware of this problem on her credit report and even offered to pay everything off to wipe the slate clean. Lucy was reluctant to do this.

She wanted to know what she could do to make the ex-boyfriend pay these accounts. I told her there was nothing she could do. The creditors viewed her as the primary person responsible for the payment. If she and her husband wanted to buy a home and use Lucy's income to help qualify, the accounts needed to be paid off. Lucy was backed into a corner. In order to buy a home, she and her husband had to make a decision. Her options were limited.

Frankly, I never advise co-signing or opening up a credit card account for someone else. Your signature implies financial accountability, and that's exactly what you'll get from disgruntled creditors if the other person becomes delinquent on the accounts. Most of the time, you're the last one to find out.

Don't take out credit for a boyfriend. Even if you think he is the one you're going to marry. You don't have the ring on your finger or the marriage license in front of you! Be responsible to yourself and protect your own credit. You may not always be single. However, nothing lets you sleep easier at night than knowing your own financial security is safe and sound.

MARRIED WOMEN

Don't think that once you're married, personal financial responsibility flies out the window. If you are going to be successful in working financially with your spouse, it's important that both of you openly communicate with each other. Secrets—especially financial ones—always have a way of being discovered. Be honest. Come up with a plan that helps the two of you succeed financially. None of us likes to think an emergency or a disaster can happen, but it can. Too often, that's when some women realize that they really needed to be more involved with the finances.

BARB'S STORY

Barb called me to see if there was any way that she and her husband could qualify for a home. They had recently filed for bankruptcy.

Barb told me that her husband Sam took care of paying all the bills. She had never questioned his ability to do this, because she trusted him. Sam started to fall behind in making the payments but never told Barb. Barb said, "Sam was just trying to protect me and didn't want me to worry."

Sam fell further and further behind and one day announced to Barb that they would have to file for bankruptcy. Barb was totally surprised. She had no idea all these financial problems were occurring. Sam had been trying to fix everything so she would never find out or worry about the circumstances he was now facing.

My first thought was, "How could you go through a relationship and not see you were slowly drowning?" Then my concern was how Barb could continue to look at the situation and only see "Sam protecting her." Protecting her from what? Her credit reports were ruined as a result of his protection. If Sam had told her what was happening from the beginning, perhaps they could have come to a mutual decision and sought outside help.

Before they could even think about buying a home, they needed to re-evaluate their communication skills and set up a plan to rebuild their credit and their relationship. The trust was already gone, and it would take some time to rebuild it.

Creditors and collection agencies are in the business of collecting money. They will use any means they can, including bullying people who do not know what their rights are. In this instance Sam may have not felt the pressure to file for bankruptcy had he known his rights under the Fair Debt Collections Practices Act.

The moral of the story? Know your rights. You never know what can happen with your finances, and had Barb known what their rights were, she may have been able to divert Sam from his decision to declare bankruptcy. It's far better to be prepared so you can protect yourself in times of trouble. If you don't know what your rights are, communicate and find out. Do not hesitate to seek outside professional help. You can always find a solution, no matter how impossible the situation may seem.

COUPLES AND MONEY

Research shows that couples fight over money a lot. Sometimes, the fighting is about control. Other times, disagreements arise from differing perspectives regarding money. One partner may be a saver while the other is a spender. Without a genuine examination of their differences, most couples simply wind up bickering, never really achieving a satisfying solution. The argument goes away until the next money incident flares up, and the cycle starts all over again. Believe it or not, there is another way.

MONEY TALKS

Rather than argue or avoid money management discussions altogether, strive to communicate with each other. Set aside time to rationally discuss your financial situation. Probably a candlelit dinner wouldn't be the best setting, but setting an appointment with each other for this discussion is valuable. This may take some time and effort and be somewhat uncomfortable, but it's well worth it. Talking gets things out in the open and can help resolve issues, rather than create frustration or anger.

Share your concerns about issues that don't seem to go away. Does one partner spend without thinking? Create a budget together and then track your progress. Create mutual goals. Instead of thinking singly, learn how to take financial advantage of being a couple.

Make sure you both know how much money is in your checking account and savings account. This will avoid a confrontation as to "Where did our money go?" It's not uncommon for the spouse who is turning over the paycheck to the other to feel frustrated when you announce, "We're short on money." The reason for the frustration is that the one who is paying the bills knows what the balance is. The other spouse who just turns in the paycheck doesn't see the outlay of bills and can't understand where the money went. Be open and review your bills and balances together.

IT TAKES TWO

Here are some smart strategies to help you and your partner handle your money more wisely. First, be proactive together. Don't rely on the other to handle it all. This scenario is unhealthy and sets one partner up for potential disaster (remember Barb's story?).

You can benefit from this mutual approach. Did you know that combining some of your money resources could result in receiving a higher interest rate? Banks frequently offer free checking or other such perks for accounts with higher balances. That's a positive thing.

You can also enhance your credit worthiness for those major life purchases such as buying a home or automobile. Two solid credit ratings and a minimum of debt can give you a lot of buying power when wielded wisely. It can also help rebuild a faulty credit report.

GET ORGANIZED TOGETHER

It's best to set up a regular time to discuss money and finances. Gather all the bills and statements. Make a list of all your assets and debts. Organize this paperwork. Make sure you have a mutual understanding of the system. It's very important that each partner know where important materials are in case of an emergency. Both partners should also have a good understanding of your true financial picture.

Share your financial goals, prioritize them, and then establish how you both want to achieve them. Pool your assets. Share a joint household account and mutually track the progress of your budget. Designate a set amount to savings and have it immediately deducted from your paychecks. Decide on what you want to save for together. When you're both openly working on a common goal, it's easier to act in unison. Teamwork is a powerful tool.

BETTY AND DAN'S STORY

I received a call one day. Betty was in a panic. She wanted to know if she could get a consolidation loan without her husband's knowledge. She had run up their credit cards with over $23,000 worth of debt. Betty's husband Dan had assumed that Betty had been making the monthly payments all along, but she hadn't. Creditors had already started calling. Dan's credit rating was destroyed, and he didn't even know about it.

We came up with a plan to help Dan and Betty get out of debt. In the meantime Betty had confided to me that she was unhappy in her marriage. She'd charged Dan's credit cards up to their limits just to get back at him. Shortly after telling me this, Betty told Dan how she felt. This became a turning point in their married life. He realized that there had been no communication between them about their finances. He'd never even taken the time to go over them with her. Suddenly Dan understood how important it was for both of them to be involved with the household finances.

Betty and Dan's situation was pretty extreme, but fortunately they were able to work things out. You can avoid this situation by communicating openly about your finances. Doing so may help your marriage to withstand financial problems that arise. Keep in mind that you're both human. Consistently do your best to talk about money and bills, and share the responsibility of managing them together.

However, don't overlook retaining a bit of financial independence. Many couples have been successful with maintaining personal accounts and limiting the money you put in them to cover personal expenses. He may want to spend some of his personal budget on season football tickets, while she may opt to purchase some software. Neither of you may understand the other's "need" for such expenses. Having your own personal accounts takes that into consideration and relieves you of disagreeing over it. Plus, the core household budget is safe from such expenses.

It's a good idea to keep separate credit cards, too. Should anything happen to your spouse, each one of you has your own credit history. Open up two to three lines of credit. Use one for household expenses, but keep the other accounts for major purchases and emergencies. Strive to keep your debt down, and agree to pay off the balances each month or as soon as you can. Establish spending limits and stick to them. Maintaining this one area of your financial life will significantly decrease your potential for arguing.

COMMON GOALS

Smart couples consider their financial future together. It's just not enough to concern yourselves with the here and now. What about retirement? Rather than relying solely on a savings account, explore other means to make your money grow. IRA's and 401(k) plans are excellent financial options, because you can claim tax deductions for every year you make a contribution. If one of you happens to be a stay-at-home type, the other can contribute to a separate/spousal IRA account.

Investing should be a shared venture as well. It may take some discussion, because the two of you may have very different approaches to investment. One may wish to play it safe, while the other wants to take high risks. Many financial advisers will tell you to combine the two approaches. Create a portfolio of savings, mutual funds, and stocks. Cover all of your financial bases. Try developing a passion for generating wealth. Maybe one of you researches new stocks and tracks the market, and the other is the savings whiz whose knowledge of various types of accounts maximizes your returns in that area. Feel free to be creative about your finances and share your victories together.

ADDITIONAL INCOME

We all experience sudden windfalls of money. As a couple decide how you'll divvy yours up before they come in. For example, you receive a large bonus from work. The two of you have already decided that one-third of that money will automatically go toward paying down your credit debt. Some will go towards a pleasant experience (because it's important to have some fun together) like a vacation. And the rest of the money will go into savings.

Having this type of plan in place can prevent you from just blowing the money and then having nothing to show for it. The same plan goes for tax refunds, prizes, and inheritance money. If the two of you simply can't decide what to do with the additional money, set it aside in a money market account or a one- to two-month CD. It'll earn you more interest than if you put it into a regular savings account.

WE'RE GETTING DIVORCED

Money problems are one of the top three reasons for marital disagreements. It is often a factor when people get divorced. Approximately 50 percent of all marriages end in divorce. If you're the "average" woman, post-divorce, you'll experience a 26 percent decline in your income. Not to mention all the emotional trauma and stress you undergo during divorce proceedings.

Knowing a few things about your finances in a time like this is critical. Before all is said and done, there will be a number of financial moves that you must undertake. First, decide who is going to pay the bills. You'll need to contact your creditors and tell them about the divorce. If you don't cancel any of the joint accounts the two of you have shared, you both may be liable for the outstanding balances. Creditors must authorize any release agreement and, at their discretion, remove the spouse who is no longer responsible for payment.

Even though the court may state your spouse is responsible for paying the joint accounts, if your name is listed on the account, the creditor will still seek payment from you should your spouse default. That is why you must contact the creditor immediately to try and remove your name from the account. While a judge may appoint your husband to make the payments on your accounts, this is no guarantee that your ex-husband will follow through. Take care of you and your own needs. Make sure your name is taken off the joint accounts.

I strongly suggest getting outside professional help when going through a divorce. Get advice on your rights from experts. Also, find out what your own obligations are. Three resources to turn to in this time are:

- A local attorney who specializes in divorce (for legal questions)

- An accountant (for tax issues)

- A Certified Divorce Planner (an expert in divorce finances)

Securing your own financial future is very important at this time. Gather up all the household financial paperwork. You'll use these materials to help you ascertain what your true financial needs are when it comes to decisions on support and division of property. Take nothing for granted.

If you end up with the house, be sure to obtain a quit claim deed from your husband. This deed will formally recognize the property transfer and take his name off the title. This deed must be recorded at the county clerk's office. Work with your attorney to ensure that all agreements are duly noted and carried out. Do not sit back and expect others to come up with a fair settlement for you. Communicate your expectations and needs so that your future is properly taken care of.

Sandy's Story

Sandy had been divorced for three years. The divorce settlement had directed her husband to pay the credit card bills. Sandy tried to purchase a car and was denied the credit. When she received a copy of her credit report, she was shocked to see that not only did her ex-husband use the credit cards for purchases after the divorce, but he had also quit paying on them. Sandy was shocked and called the credit card company to have the items removed from her credit card.

The credit card company informed Sandy that since her name was still on the credit card and she was a joint borrower, she was responsible for the payments. Even with the court settlement, the credit card company would not remove the information. This could have been avoided had she immediately closed the credit card accounts back when the divorce was still pending. At the very least, she should have made sure that her name was taken off the accounts. This was a hard lesson to learn.

WRAP-UP

We should all be proactive and in charge of our financial lifestyles. Be patient with yourself. Allow both you and your money to grow. It's true that money won't buy you happiness or love, but it can offer some security and allow you to enjoy your life. Like anything, your money requires time and attention. Give yourself the gift of personal financial security. Share what you know with others if you can. In the long run, you'll be proud of what you have accomplished and hopefully living well off of it, too.

COACH'S TIP

Select one money tradition that has prevented you from pursuing financial security. Focus on transforming that belief into a myth.

18

A House, a Car,
Dreams Come True

Major purchases, such as buying a home or an automobile, are important experiences in one's financial life. Although such dreams may seem unattainable, with some careful long-term planning, you can qualify for a loan that will enable you to buy that home or car or whatever you wish to purchase. If you understand how to properly apply for credit and have a sound credit rating, you can achieve your dreams.

BEFORE YOU APPLY

Every industry has its own language. When you're new to a certain industry, it can be difficult to understand what's being said because you're not familiar with the terminology. Here are some standard terms that you'll need to know when applying for a mortgage:

- *Term of loan*—the time it will take to pay off the mortgage. Generally the industry standard is thirty years, but you can find fifteen- and twenty-five year options too.

- *Fixed rate*—your interest rate will remain the same throughout the life of the mortgage.

- *Adjustable rate mortgage* (ARM)—initially your interest rate will start out low, often one to two points lower than a fixed rate (based upon the current economy). Rates are then adjusted; the terms of the loan set forth a timetable. Most rate adjustments occur between six and twelve months. The benefit of adjusted rates is that if market rates fall, so will your monthly payment.

- *Rate cap*—with an ARM, it's typical to establish a cap, or how high your rate can adjust within a given period as well as over the life of the loan. This cap protects you against drastic market changes, but an ARM is not as stable as a fixed rate.

- *Rate reduction*—you can reduce your interest rate by opting for a shorter-term loan. A fifteen-year rate is often 0.25 to 0.5 percent lower than a thirty-year rate. You'll also pay less in the long run because you'll pay less interest (even with the same amount) due to the shorter loan length.

- *Prepayment penalty*—if there is a prepayment penalty on your loan, it will be disclosed in the note you sign with the lender. You will have to pay a penalty if you prepay the loan balance before a certain period of time (mentioned in your note). The penalty could be six months' interest of your loan. Again, the note will state it.

Let's say your loan has a three-year prepayment penalty. If you pay off the loan during the first three years of the loan, you pay a penalty. After the three-year period, there is no longer a prepayment penalty. Seek loans without prepayment penalties unless you know you'll have the loan for a longer period and you can get a better interest rate by having it.

RESEARCH YOUR LENDER

Before you actually submit an application, do your homework. Decide what type of loan for a mortgage will best suit your needs. Determine what qualifications the lender will be looking for. By doing some investigation beforehand, you can increase your chances of approval by making sure your application complies with the creditor's criteria and it is complete. Contact the bank or mortgage company, and find out which credit bureau it uses. Is it Equifax, Experian, or Trans Union? Many lenders will run all three credit reports and merge them. FICO scores are important in qualifying for a mortgage. Ask the lender how high your FICO score must be to get the best interest rates and how low it can be to qualify.

KNOW YOUR CREDIT REPORT!

Once you know which reporting bureau is used, request a copy of your credit report that shows your FICO score. Review it for inaccuracies and for any potential weaknesses. Should you need to clean up any errors, you'll have time to do so. If you have one negative entry among many positive entries, the one negative shouldn't hurt your chances of being approved for credit. Check how high your FICO score is and what you can do to improve it.

EXCESSIVE INQUIRIES

Creditors prefer not to see a lot of account inquiries on your credit report. One way to avoid this is to carry a clean, updated copy of your report with you. When speaking with a prospective lender (remember you still haven't applied yet), you can refer to this report. The lender or mortgage company can evaluate your rating on the spot and indicate whether your application would be approved. At that time you can go ahead and grant authorization to run a credit check.

SAFETY TIP

Never give your information to anyone over the telephone! This information is personal, and you should take utmost care to preserve it. Someone who asks you for it can run a credit check, which will end up appearing on your credit record. You want to avoid this, so play it safe and provide such information only when you're ready to personally authorize a credit check.

SHOPPING AROUND FOR A LENDER

Traditional places to seek a mortgage loan are local banks, credit unions, and mortgage companies. However, you should be aware that numerous institutions offer home mortgage loans, and it's best to shop around and find the best deal for you. Institutions that offer mortgages include banks, savings and loans, mutual savings banks, mortgage companies, mortgage broker, and credit unions.

Most banks, savings and loans, and mortgage companies are referred to as direct lenders. Mortgage brokers represent a number of lenders offering a loan product. Their services can often be found on the Internet or in local offices.

WHAT'S THE DIFFERENCE?

Direct lenders, such as banks, will make you an offer based on their services. A broker will make you an offer drawing upon several sources.

Because of the number of sources to which the broker has access, this is called unbiased advice; with a direct lender, it's considered biased advice. Some experts say that a mortgage broker seeks to get you the best loan for your particular needs and is not restricted by any one lender establishment's policies and terms.

If your application is denied, you'll need to begin the loan process all over again with another direct lender. With a mortgage broker, if one lender turns down your loan, there's a chance that another lender might approve your application without your having to reapply.

COMPLETING YOUR APPLICATION

The loan process is the same for a purchase of a home as well as a refinance.

All lenders require you to fill out a standardized application, frequently referred to as a 1003 (a Fannie Mae designation). Your application should reflect current and complete information. Items on your credit report should confirm information you note on your application. It's possible that a creditor will not call to confirm every bit of information on your application, but most do. You'll be denied credit if they discover you've listed false or inaccurate information on your application. Be prepared to provide the following:

- W-2s for the past two years
- Year-to-date pay stubs
- Current debt information (account numbers, balances, creditors' addresses)
- The purchase contract for the home you want to buy
- Tax returns for the past two years

- Bank statements for the past three months

- Any statements for a 401(k) or IRA accounts, or other investment information listing assets

- Copy of divorce papers; documents about child support and alimony

- Copies of any past bankruptcy papers

WHAT TYPE OF INFORMATION WILL THEY ASK FOR?

No matter what type of loan you apply for, you'll have to fill out a number of forms, including an initial loan application, verification of employment, and verification of deposit. Your loan qualification depends upon these forms, so make sure they're complete and accurate. A lender will confirm the information you've given. You'll be asked to list all of your assets: property, cars, furniture, jewelry, silver, and so on. You'll also need to mention any liabilities, debts, or outstanding obligations. If you have debt that will be paid off within ten months, in most instances, a lender won't consider these entries.

Tell the lender about any past problems with your credit. Be honest. You don't want the lender to find out such information on its own, which will lead to a credit denial. Communication is essential. It's possible that an explanation letter can clear up a negative entry on your credit report. Unlike a credit card, a mortgage has loan security—the house itself. This makes it a bit easier to get approval.

PAST BANKRUPTCY?

If it has been at least two years since your bankruptcy was discharged and you've established new credit, you could qualify for a loan. Your new credit should be good, and no negative entries should appear on your report since the bankruptcy.

EMPLOYMENT VERIFICATION

A lender will look for certain factors when reviewing your present employment and will request a verification of employment form filled out by your employer or other authorized personnel. A lender needs to know about length of employment, base amount of pay per hour or monthly, overtime pay (if applicable), and bonuses and commissions.

Lenders prefer to see that you've spent at least two years with the same employer. However, if you've been employed with a new company for only four months but your current job is similar or the same type of work that you did at your previous position, lenders may regard this record as acceptable. Lenders can send verification forms to other employers you've had within the past two years.

Lenders will regard positively a change in position to better yourself financially. On the other hand, having breaks in employment every couple of months and switching business fields will raise flags to lenders. They may ask you questions about the stability of your employment or may request a letter of explanation from you. Different lenders' practices vary. Just be honest with your lender, and explain your situation clearly and concisely.

NO BIG CHANGES

While you're going through the process of approval and up until the time funds are disbursed, do not make any changes to your financial situation. For instance, don't open a department store credit line, don't purchase a major new appliance for the new house, don't buy a new car, and don't quit your job. Such changes, though seemingly innocent, will cause the lender to ask questions and may result in withdrawal of your loan approval.

It's not unusual for a lender to request a credit report and make a final check with your employer one last time before granting and funding your loan. Play it safe and avoid making any financial changes during this delicate processing time.

HEIDI'S STORY

Heidi was in the process of refinancing her home. Because of some past credit problems, we were having a hard time placing her with a loan company. At last I found a lender that would refinance the property with good rates.

While we were shopping around to find the best lender for Heidi, the family car broke down, and Heidi and her husband decided to lease a new car. I was never informed about the new lease. When the lender pulled another credit report, the lease payment of $499 showed up. Heidi and her husband could not qualify for the loan because this new payment increased their debt ratios for qualification.

It was several months before Heidi and her husband could reapply for the loan and successfully be approved. They had to pay down some of their debts to get their debt ratios in line.

DEPOSIT VERIFICATION

This form will be mailed to your bank (or banks) that you've listed as a source of down payment on your application. The bank will indicate your current balance, along with your average daily balance, then return this form to the mortgage company.

When applying for a home loan, you will not be allowed to borrow money for your down payment or your closing costs. It's best to have this money already saved up.

Should you fall short of the down payment, a lender may allow you to borrow that money from a relative as long as the person provides you with what is called a gift letter. Your relative then writes a letter or signs a statement informing the lender that the money is a gift and will not require repayment.

HOW THE MORTGAGE AMOUNT IS CALCULATED

A lender will want to know how much money you want to borrow, the value of the property, and your financial situation. This information will help the lender determine what the maximum amount of your loan will be.

The appraisal opinion will weigh heavily in the lender's mind in determining whether you qualify for the amount you seek. Generally lenders will offer a certain percentage of the property value, such as 80 to 95 percent. You will be expected to make up the rest of the amount with a down payment. Some companies offer 100 percent financing, but you must have a high FICO score.

PROPERTY APPRAISAL

The lender will require an appraisal of the property. Basically a real estate appraiser will examine the property and issue a report on the property value. When you first submit your application, you'll be asked for a check to cover processing fees. This check covers two things: the fee to obtain your credit report and the appraiser's fee. Both fees are nonrefundable.

What will the appraiser look for? The appraiser will compare your property to other homes in the area and conduct a market study to determine the property value. Ideally the appraisal should be close to the selling price.

WHAT IF THE APPRAISAL IS LOWER THAN THE SELLING PRICE?

A lender will offer only a percentage of the property-appraised value. In this situation you can do one of two things. You can pay more than the appraised value, which means you'll have to pay a larger down payment to make up for the difference between the price of the house and its appraised value. Or you can renegotiate with the seller. If the seller does not wish to renegotiate, you are not obligated to finalize the sale. The reason is that the sale was based on the original price and not the appraised value.

WHAT IF THE APPRAISAL IS HIGHER THAN THE SELLING PRICE?

In this instance the original sales price remains the same. The lender will base the down payment on the selling price. Appraisals are rarely valued above the selling price because the appraiser knows what this amount is prior to making the appraisal.

THE TOTAL PACKAGE

After the credit reports have been checked, the employment and deposit verifications have been processed, and the appraisal has been received by the lender, your loan package is submitted to an underwriter or the loan company for final approval.

When you file your application, ask your lender how long the approval process may take. Factors that can affect processing include the complexity of your mortgage, current market conditions, and the need for additional information. Typically decisions are made within 48-72 hours once the lender has received all the pertinent paperwork and information. Some loans may take longer.

THE FOUR-TO-ONE RULE

When you're trying to qualify for your house payment, use the general rule of four to one. That is, your monthly payment should not exceed 25 percent of your gross monthly income.

Here's an example. Your house payment is $500 each month. Thus, your gross monthly income should be at least $2,000. Be aware that different lenders have their own practices and may use another ratio. Some may be higher. Feel free to ask your lender about how it calculates the ratio when you apply.

MY LOAN APPLICATION WAS DENIED

Federal law requires a lender to inform you in writing of the specific reasons for the denial of your loan application. You need to understand why your application was denied. You may be able to find answers or explanations or other alternatives that will satisfy the lender's standards. If you cannot resolve these issues with the current lender, you may be able to enhance your chances of approval with another lender.

Certain factors can affect a loan decision:

Your down payment. Is the proposed amount enough? If it isn't, can the lender suggest other types of mortgages that you could qualify for based on a lower down payment?

The appraisal. Consider the appraised value of the property. Are your mortgage amount requirements too high based upon the appraisal? It's possible that the agent undervalued your property. Check similar houses in the neighborhood to see if they've been sold at comparable prices. You can then suggest that the lender reexamine the appraisal. You are entitled to a copy of the appraisal if you were charged fees for it.

Your past credit history. Sometimes a lender may question your ability to make your monthly payments based on prior credit history. How do your debt ratios compare with the lender's standards? If the concerns involve a specific rating and special circumstances were involved, you may be asked to explain these circumstances.

YOUR RIGHTS

Federal law protects all potential home buyers from discrimination based on race, color, national origin, religion, sex, marital status, age, receipt of public assistance funds, familial status (you have children under eighteen), disability, or the exercise of any other consumer protection right under the law.

None of the above-listed factors may be taken into consideration when a lender reviews your application. A lender cannot discourage you from loan application based upon your gender or marital status. A lender must offer you the same credit terms as another applicant who has a similar loan request.

The Fair Housing Act and the Equal Credit Opportunity Act provide you with these rights. Visit the Federal Trade Commission Web site (www.ftc.gov) for free copies of these acts.

I WANT TO REFINANCE MY HOME

Basically the application process is the same as that for a regular mortgage. There are several programs, so you'll need to check with your lender. For example, a second trust deed may allow you to take 100 to 125 percent of the appraised property value; an equity line of credit can offer similar percentages.

There are various reasons to refinance. You may be able to take advantage of lower interest rates, to lower your monthly payment, or you may wish to consolidate your debts into your mortgage payment, which will save you money. Whatever your situation, you need to do your homework and find the best deal to suit your particular needs. In the refinancing of your home, your loan costs are added into the loan.

BUYING AN AUTOMOBILE

You're ready to trade in your present vehicle. Will you purchase a new car or a used car? Or maybe you'll lease? The decision is up to you.

Research your options. Buying a car is a major purchase, second to buying a home, so be well informed. More than likely you can't afford to buy a car outright, and you'll need to be approved for financing. The financing/credit process is pretty much the same as that for buying a house. You fill out a lot of paperwork, and a credit check is done.

HOW MUCH WILL THE CAR REALLY COST?

Once you've selected a model or type of car, figure out how much it's going to cost you. Don't rely solely on the sticker price. Consider closing costs such as license fees, loan or lease fees, sales tax, and the cost of registration. Add basic use costs, such as insurance, maintenance, repairs, gas, and parking.

When you come up with a solid figure, look at your financial situation. Can you realistically afford the car you've selected? Refer to your budget. How much of a car payment can you make without overextending yourself financially?

If you can afford the automobile of your choice, terrific. If not, save some money. In either case your best option is to make a large down payment, which will lower the amount of interest you'll pay over the life of the loan.

YOUR CREDIT APPLICATION

When you fill out a loan application, the lender will consider your debt to income ratio. Most banks will offer loan packages to people whose debt is between 35 and 38 percent of their income. This is not a hard-and-fast rule, however. Because you want to keep credit inquiries to a minimum, check with the finance manager at the car dealership before submitting an application to determine the criteria for loan qualification. You can also hand carry a recent copy of your credit report with you. Just be sure to protect your information. If you give it to a dealer, chances are, the finance manager will run a check. Too many recent credit inquiries from shopping around will only create credit approval problems for you.

Expect the car dealership's finance department to examine your income, employment, residency, and prior credit history. The car dealership will look closely at your car payment history and your FICO score too.

Review your credit reports before your car search. Why? Your APR will be based on your credit score. You want the lowest interest rates you can find. In addition to shopping around for the best deal, make sure your application looks good.

UNDERSTAND ALL THE TERMS

When you work with a dealer, understand what you're paying for and why. Don't be afraid to ask questions. For instance, if you're required to put down a deposit, find out whether it's refundable.

Likewise, if you have any questions or concerns regarding your contract, ask. For example, will you be assessed penalties for paying off the loan early? Clarify any information you don't understand.

Should you have any doubts about anything, get an answer before you sign any paperwork.

WRAP-UP

Big ticket items, such as a house or a car, are financial milestones in a woman's life. Don't be intimidated by the cost of these purchases. Map out your dreams. Once you decide to take action, focus on achieving your goal. If you feel unsure about what you're setting out to do, talk with people. You'll be surprised at how many people will share their "war stories" about buying a home or car with you. Often their experiences can help you learn about the process. Take advantage of books, magazines, and Web sites so you know what to ask and watch out for.

You are capable of making your dreams come true. Only you can determine what they are and then work at making them a reality.

COACH'S TIP

Once your car is paid off pay cash for your next car, take the money you were making on car payments, and put it in a special account. Let the money build up so that when it is time to purchase a new car, you will be able to pay cash and need no financing help.

19

Watching Your
Wealth Grow

Too many women don't know what is available to them for financial planning and saving for their future, let alone the definition of the terms and types of accounts that are out there. We don't have time to sift through all the information available.

In this chapter I will help you get a better understanding of the functions of the basic accounts you hear and read about.

Many credit unions and lending institutions have financial advisers who can help you with the decisions you need to make regarding your accounts. But you must understand your options and what these financial terms mean.

COMPOUND INTEREST

If you are in your twenties, you have the time to see the power of compounding. For example, if you start saving $2,000.00 ($166.66 per month) a year at age twenty-five and keep it up until you reach the age of thirty-five, and never add another penny to the account, based on 10 percent annual growth, at age sixty-five you'll have

$204,572.00 saved. The growth comes from compounding the interest and principal.

At age forty-five you will have to save $3,500 a year for twenty years to save the same amount.

If you are in your forties or fifties and need to make up for lost time, start saving as much as possible by putting money into tax-deferred savings plans and other accounts.

CERTIFICATE OF DEPOSIT (CD)

A CD is a guaranteed interest rate made on a deposit at your credit union or lending institution for a specific number of months. For example, the CD may be for a term of three months, one year, or three years. If you withdraw the money early, you will be subject to a penalty. It is FDIC insured.

MONEY MARKET ACCOUNT (MMA)

This account is sponsored by a credit union or bank. You have access to your money in this account whenever you need it without any penalties. The interest rates will fluctuate according to the current interest rates.

Talk to an adviser at your bank or credit union to evaluate what type of account is best for your situation.

RETIREMENT ACCOUNTS

You have a lot to consider when planning for your retirement. In addition to figuring out your needs, there are a number of ways to allocate your money. You'll want to investigate each of the retirement options so that you can come up with a plan that builds income efficiently and wisely.

When you're building your retirement savings, it's worth your while to look into tax-advantaged investing. There are two ways to do this: tax-deferred programs and pretax programs. Essentially "tax-advantaged" translates into account strategies that don't require you to pay taxes until you withdraw the money or allow you to lower your income taxes. Before signing up for an account, do a bit of research and crunch some numbers to see which programs are appropriate for you and your needs.

IRAS

IRAs (individual retirement accounts) offer tax-deductible contributions and tax-deferred savings. There are different types of IRAs:

- Traditional deductible IRA

- Traditional nondeductible IRA

- SEP IRA

- Roth IRA

The two traditional IRAs and SEP IRA are tax-deferred. You will owe no tax until you withdraw your money. The Roth IRA, on the other hand, is tax-free, providing you follow all the withdrawal rules for the type of account. It allows your money to accumulate without owing taxes, even when you choose to make withdrawals.

The one requirement to opening up an IRA account is that you must have earned income, in other words, money paid to you for work services you performed. You can contribute only a maximum amount annually as long as you don't contribute more than you earn. Since the maximum amount is subject to change, check with the person who prepares your taxes or your financial adviser for the amount you may contribute.

The SEP IRA (simplified employee pension) is for the self-employed person or small business. It allows higher deposits to be made annually than an IRA. The money also grows tax-deferred.

The Roth IRA is similar to the traditional IRA, except that the annual contribution is not tax deductible. Upon your retirement and withdrawal of the Roth IRA, the money is tax-free.

Basically with a traditional tax-deductible IRA, you are able to take immediate advantage of tax savings once you contribute. Your account earnings are also tax-deferred. However, should you need to withdraw from this account, you will have to pay taxes.

The traditional nondeductible IRA offers tax-deferred account earnings. This account itself is not tax deductible, and you will be required to pay taxes at regular rates when you withdraw from it.

Benefits of the Roth IRA include tax-free income and no required withdrawals. To qualify for tax-free withdrawal, your account must be opened for at least five years.

SEPARATE SPOUSAL ACCOUNTS

If one spouse works while the other stays home, you are eligible to contribute money to a separate spousal account. The benefit is that the stay-at-home partner can build an individual retirement fund. This is a terrific opportunity for married couples and is definitely worth taking advantage of.

Several online sites provide retirement calculators:

- financialmuse.com
- about.com (visit the money and finance section)

By calculating different scenarios, you'll be able to see which account is right for you.

OPENING AN IRA ACCOUNT

Here's the easy part. Select a bank, a brokerage firm, mutual fund company, or another financial institution you want to work with. Apply for an IRA by completing the application form. The institution you select will be referred to as the "custodian" or the "trustee" of your IRA account.

IRA accounts are self-directed; that is, you're responsible for deciding how the money is to be invested. You're also responsible for adhering to account rules; for example, you can only contribute within the guidelines set forth. Annual investments also need to be guideline-approved. All contributions must be reported to the IRS. If your contributions are tax deductible, you can do this on your federal tax return. Otherwise, you'll need to fill out a Form 8606 for non-tax-deductible contributions.

IRA INVESTMENTS

I mentioned that IRAs are self-directed. You will have to figure out how you want your contributions directed: regular savings accounts, stocks, bonds, mutual funds, and so on. According to federal guidelines, you are not able to invest in collectibles, fine art, gems, or non-U.S. coins. Account guidelines provide that you can buy and sell investments without paying taxes on any gains.

WHEN CAN I MAKE AN IRA CONTRIBUTION?

If you'd like to make an IRA contribution for the previous tax year, you need to open the account by April 15. You can take advantage of spreading out your IRA deposit over a fifteen-month period by having a standard amount deducted from your checking account and deposited into your IRA as of January 2. Chances are, you won't feel the financial pinch as much as you would by opting to make a lump sum deposit closer to the April 15 deadline. If you know that you're not a disciplined saver, choose to spread out your contributions. That way, you'll be building your retirement income steadily and you'll be less likely to put off your contribution.

401(K)S AND 403(B)S

These retirement programs are offered by your employers, 401(k)s by companies and 403(b)s by nonprofit organizations (charitable organizations, universities, some hospitals, etc). These plans allow you to defer taxes on a portion of your salary by selecting to make an authorized contribution to your employer's program.

Contributions are typically a percentage of your paycheck. If the amount is deducted through a paycheck reduction, the contribution is considered pretax. The federal government has specific limits about much you can contribute to your plan. Most employers will allow you to contribute up to the limit.

Your contribution earnings will grow tax-deferred. Taxes will not be assessed until you withdraw the money for retirement. Note that these plans are *tax-deferred*, not tax-free. The amount of money you contribute is not reported on your W-2, which reduces your income and may affect your tax bracket.

To apply for a savings account, check with your employer. If it offers a plan, then you'll need to sign off on an election form. This form authorizes the paycheck deductions that will be your plan contribution. You will also need to decide whether you want to select different investments or opt for investor packages determined by your employer.

OTHER BENEFITS

Some employers offer company match programs. For every employee dollar, the employer matches the contribution with additional money, generally a predetermined percentage. This is a wonderful opportunity to enhance your retirement dollars. You're already contributing your own money, but having additional money provided is just like getting free money!

Sometimes employers allow you to take out loans based on your 401(k) plan. Loan repayment must be made on a regular basis and is usually figured at market rates. In this instance, you are not taxed on the money nor is the loan considered a withdrawal. In some instances, you may make a withdrawal due to a hardship, such as a medical emergency, college tuition or a payment related to your home. This rule also applies for IRAs.

Otherwise, should you withdraw funds from your 401(k) plan and you are younger than 59 1/2, you will have to pay early withdrawal fees. You may also forfeit the right to make contributions to your account for a set amount of time.

DIFFERENCES BETWEEN AN IRA AND A 401(K) OR 403(B)

If it's possible, you may want to take advantage of both retirement programs. However, if your budget allows you to contribute only so much, then you'll need to decide between the two. In a nutshell, here are the options for an IRA:

- Lower contribution limits

- Nearly limitless investment opportunity

- May not significantly reduce your annual income for tax purposes

With a 401(k) or 403(b), the options you have are:

- Higher contribution limits

- Company match contributions (if part of the company program)

- May significantly reduce your annual income for tax purposes

- If you change companies, you can roll over your 401(k) or 403(b) balance to another plan, to an IRA, or leave it with your previous employer (if the employer allows this)

Carefully consider all of these factors. Feel free to seek outside professional help to answer any questions. Most large companies have staff on hand to address your concerns. Smaller companies frequently hire third party administrators (TPAs) or outside financial services to assist their employees with these programs. Your employer will not make investment recommendations. You'll need to consult with the plan's financial adviser.

SHANNA'S STORY

When Shanna's husband died at middle age, she thought she was destitute, with only a $700-per-month pension to live on. As Shanna began to go through her husband's files, however, she discovered that her husband had saved more than $500,000 in a 403(b) plan. She was amazed. What Shanna didn't realize was that her husband had the contribution deducted from his paycheck first. They did indeed spend all of his paycheck, but only what was left after his pretax savings. Smart man. That is why I encourage people to pay themselves first. The rewards are worth it.

And what a great relief for Shanna! She could at last relax and know she was taken care of.

KEOGH PLANS

In the event that you are self-employed, whether full or part time, you'll want to investigate into a Keogh plan. The two types of Keogh plans are a profit-sharing plan and a money purchase plan. There are regulations associated with a Keogh plan, and one of them is that a money purchase contribution is mandatory. This contribution must be of the same percentage each year, regardless of your profits even if you made none. With a profit-sharing plan, you can change your contribution amount each year. And there is no restriction preventing you from contributing to both plans in the same year.

Keogh contributions are tax deductible. The limit on what you can contribute will depend upon the version of Keogh you select. In some instances, you'll be able to contribute 25 percent of your net income. Keogh plans are a good choice for self-employed workers because the plan allows them to set aside the largest amount of money in a retirement program, sometimes up to $30,000 a year.

Keogh earnings are also tax-deferred. Until you make your withdrawal, which is assumed to be when you retire, you will not have to pay taxes on this money. When it is time to make the withdrawal, your Keogh money will be taxed as ordinary income.

The Pros and Cons

Keogh plans allow you to make pretax contributions, which reduce your annual income and your yearly taxes. Both contributions and earnings are tax-deferred, so that's another terrific advantage to Keogh plans. Another thing, you can invest in regular IRAs too. Keogh accounts can be difficult to set up on your own because of their complexity. It's probably a good idea to work under the guidance of an expert so that you maximize your money and find a plan suited to your needs.

When Can I Contribute to a Keogh?

You can make Keogh contributions for a given tax year. However, to claim a deduction for that given tax year, your Keogh account must be opened by December 31, or if you are incorporated, by the end of your fiscal year.

WRAP-UP

Planning for your retirement requires thinking in the here and now. Most experts will tell you that the bulk of your retirement future depends on the choices and decisions you make today. Do not delay making plans and building your retirement income. There are a number of solid plans to choose from as well as a wealth of resources to help you discover what's right for you. If you're concerned that you may not make the right choice, get help. Start saving today, stay focused on your goals, and try to participate in plans that allow you to generate additional wealth through tax-advantaged investing.

Visit my web site at www.financialvictory.com for a referral of an investment adviser, financial adviser or financial planner in your area.

COACH'S TIP

Some women may be a bit reluctant to start retirement planning because of insecurities about their finances and lack of knowledge about the available options. If you feel reluctant to start saving, talk with some of your friends. See if they have a financial adviser or have started their own retirement programs. Or find a local seminar on retirement planning and attend it. Don't worry if it takes you time to understand all the ins and outs of retirement planning.

20

MONEY CALORIE COUNTER

———

This is a fun chapter. It's probably the most eye-opening one in this book as well. I'm going to show you ways to watch your money grow while saving calories.

Two topics consistently pop up in conversations: one is money, and the other is health, weight in particular if you're a woman. Life would be a whole lot easier if our bank accounts grew and our waistlines stayed in the lower-digit range. Unfortunately for many of us, the opposite holds true. But what if I told you how to save money, get rid of those extra calories, and lose some weight? Sound too good to be true? Well, it's not.

By and large, our society likes fast food for convenience as well as taste. When I was in Brazil, McDonald's had just opened up, and it was jam-packed with people. I couldn't believe it when we traveled to other countries and saw Pizza Huts along with familiar doughnut shops that we have here in the United States. It just goes to show you that people everywhere love fast food. The taste, the fat, and the sugar are a tough combination to resist. I know that if you give me a bag of fries, I'm one happy camper.

A fun part about being a woman is that we love and crave

chocolate, potato chips, ice cream, and pizza—all of which just happen to be high-calorie, great-tasting items. We can even blame PMS and pregnancy as the culprits behind our cravings. In a sense we're lucky because we can blame lots of things for our food cravings and overeating. Depression, anxiety, and stress factor into that fat-filled trip to the refrigerator, doughnut shop, or ice-cream parlor.

The downside to our love of certain tasty items is weight gain. What I'm going to show you will help you battle the bulge while making your money grow. With just a little creative thinking and some small changes in your eating habits, you can lose a few pounds and save some money. Isn't that great? You'll shrink and your money will grow! You'll be wearing a big grin as a trimmer you slinks in to the bank to deposit your extra savings.

What would you say if I told you by giving up two doughnuts a week, you could yield retirement savings of $6,552.26 in twenty years, assuming a 10 percent return? Passing up potato chips with your lunch could save $176.80 a year and produce $10,483.62 over two decades and reduce 63,232 calories a year. By eliminating the cream cheese with your bagel three times a week, you could cut 54,000 calories a year from your diet and yield an annual savings of $117.00 or $7,371.29 in twenty years. Wow!

REDUCING WHILE SAVING

Read through the Money Calorie Counter. The numbers are based on a scenario of an individual eating a selection of these items five times during the week. The chart will show you how many calories can be saved, plus how much money you can have based on savings or an investment yielding 10 percent interest compounded for ten years and twenty years.

The trick to this savings and calorie reduction plan is *not* to make the purchase. Instead take the money you'd be spending and put it into an interest-bearing account or investment. Let's follow the example of french fries (my favorite). A large order of fries costs $2.05 and contains 540 calories. If I ordered fries five days out of the week, the monthly cost would be $44.42. The calories would be 11,700. Are your eyes beginning to widen?

Let's go a step farther. If I take the savings ($44.42) every month that I would have spent on fries, and put it into an account that earns 10 percent interest compounded, in ten years, I'll have $9,099.21 in savings. In twenty years I'll have $33,731.16. The incredible thing is that that I'm avoiding 140,400 calories per year, or forty pounds. Amazing, isn't it?

MONEY CALORIE COUNTER

By cutting out about five hundred calories a day, at the end of a week you could lose one pound. Again, we're working with a proactive model (much like budgeting) of consistent small steps leading to a sizable change. How does it work? Begin by thinking about your diet. Where can you make some calorie and budget cuts?

In addition to calories cut, consider where you're putting your money. Depending upon the type of account you put your savings into, you'll accelerate your interest earnings if compounded interest is involved.

I hope you're beginning to see how tracking your calories and your savings can be an eye-opening experience. Try to make this exercise fun. See what alternatives you can come up with. It's really just a matter of altering your perspective or seeing how to modify a current standard for something that's less costly and fattening.

MONEY CALORIE COUNTER

BASED ON 5 DAYS A WEEK   10% INT. COMPOUNDED

ITEMS: Size	Cost	Srv.	CALORIES Yearly	YEARLY COST	SAVINGS 10 Years	20 Years
DOUGNUTS						
	.75	170	44,200 (13 lbs.)	$195.00	$3,318.49	$12,339.74
Cream filled						
	.75	270	70,200 (20 lbs.)	195.00	$3,318.49	$12,339.74
COOKIE						
2 ½ oz	1.39	325	84,500 (25 lbs.)	361.40	$6,180.17	$22,910.16
HAMBURGER						
	.95	270	70,200 (20 lbs.)	247.00	$4,215.71	$15,627.81
CHEESEBURGER						
	1.02	320	83,200 (23 lbs.)	265.20	$4,527.01	$16,782.05
FRIES						
Large	2.05	540	140,400 (40lbs.)	533.00	$9,099.21	$33,731.16
Medium	1.71	450	117,000 (33 lbs.)	444.60	$7,589.50	$28,134.62
PIZZA 1 slice cheese						
	2.50	309	80,340 (23lbs.)	650.00	$11,696.45	$41,135.00
MOCHA/ICED WITH WHIPPED CREAM						
16 oz	3.35	370	96,200 (27 lbs.)	871.00	$14,876.65	$55,114.99
MOCHA FRAPACINNO						
16 oz	3.33	290	75,400 (22 lbs.)	865.80	$14,779.57	$54,788.46
w/whipped cream						
		390	75,400 (22 lbs.)	865.80	$14,779.57	$54,788.46
MOCHA LATTE						
16 oz	3.05	270	70,200 (20 lbs.)	793.00	$13,536.16	$50,179.49

BASED ON 5 DAYS A WEEK					10% INT. COMPOUNDED	
ITEMS:		CALORIES		YEARLY	SAVINGS	
Size	Cost	Srv.	Yearly	COST	10 Years	20 Years
CHOCOLATE CANDY BAR						
Large	.89	510	132,600 (38 lbs.)	231.40	$3,949.41	$14,640.63
Small	.50	230	59,800 (17 lbs.)	130.00	$2,218.47	$ 8,223.96
ICE CREAM (CHOCOLATE)						
4 ½ oz	1.89	180	46,800 (13 lbs.)	491.40	$8,388.40	$31,096.15
9 oz.	3.59	360	93,600 (27 lbs.)	933.40	$15,926.70	$59,063.71
13 ½ oz	5.19	540	140,400 (40 lbs.)	1,349.40	$23,039.82	$85,391.03

WRAP-UP

Practice cutting back on as many items as you can. Start out slow, and take on one or two items each week. At the very least you'll see how you can save on favorite foods simply by purchasing them at the grocery store instead of opting to dine out or grab some fast food. Track your progress to keep yourself motivated.

And who knows? Maybe by the end of the year, you can take some of your savings and treat yourself to clothing that's a size smaller. Wouldn't that be nice?

COACH'S TIP

The next time you're asked if you want to supersize your meal, say, "No." Most restaurant and fast-food portions are much larger than a normal serving—meaning that you're eating more than is necessary. The price quoted may sound like a deal, but you've just been talked into an "up sale." Opt for the smallest size—it's fewer calories and costs less.

21

MONEY-MAKING ACCOUNTS

W hen you say the word investing, most women get a blank look on their faces. The word is intimidating. Why? Because it has been a "man thing," or many women have regarded investing as risky. Another reason for this hesitancy is not understanding the vocabulary and terms associated with investing. If you don't understand the terms or vocabulary, how could you possibly feel comfortable making an investment?

I don't profess to be an investment adviser or an investment counselor. I am not trained in that manner, nor do I have a license to operate as a financial Wall Street guru. My husband, Hal, is a financial adviser with the required licenses so he is my expert for investment knowledge and advice.

But I do know that investing is a serious matter. If you don't have an adviser to help you, and you try to do it on your own, you run a risk. Let me share a story with you to show you what I mean.

PAUL AND JOAN'S STORY

Joan called my office to see if I could help her with refinancing of their home. She wanted to take out equity from her home to pay off all her credit card debt, which totaled more than $35,000. It was obvious that she and her husband, Paul, were having problems making ends meet. Lucky for them, they had enough equity in their home to pull out that much cash to pay off the bills.

As we were completing the transaction, Joan told me that her husband had been taking cash advances from their credit cards to do day trading on the Internet. He had no experience investing, and instead of growing the money, he lost it all.

Paul kept thinking that if he continued to take out cash advances, he would eventually make a return on his money. But he was wrong. He just about bankrupted his household. And Paul was doing the trading in secret.

When Joan found out about his reckless behavior, she canceled many of her credit cards so Paul couldn't use them. Needless to say, an ugly situation developed between Paul and Joan. Paul finally owned up to his problem and canceled the remaining credit cards.

By refinancing their house to pay off the debts, they basically have little equity left in the home, and if this problem recurs, Paul and Joan could end up bankrupt.

The moral of this story is that many people go online to do day trading. It becomes addictive, like gambling. If you don't know what you're doing, see a financial adviser or financial planner to help you make the right choices and set up a financial plan that will grow your wealth for the future.

MORE WOMEN ARE CURIOUS ABOUT INVESTING

Lately a number of women have become more interested in investing. This is a good thing. Women must learn how to invest their hard-earned money because investing creates wealth. It's a way to make your money work for you, and the returns can be quite rewarding.

Most experts agree that you should have a mix of stocks, bonds, and cash in your financial plan. Through wise investment, you can generate the wealth you need to fund your dreams and retirement years.

Nevertheless, the majority of women do not invest, most likely because of certain misconceptions. Some may think that they don't have enough money to invest, but they're wrong. There are investments that can be purchased for $25 a month. Also, by brown bagging your lunch, you can come up with enough savings, at least $2,000 a year, to put toward investments. Allocating a certain portion of your budget, say 5 to 10 percent, can help you come up with the additional money you need to begin investing.

Women may avoid investing because they feel they don't understand how the market works. They may be intimidated by the financial world in general. However, there are more opportunities for women to learn now than ever before. You can attend a seminar, join an investment club, read up on financial planning in books and magazines, and consult financial experts and online sources. Understanding the basic principles of investing can give you the confidence you need to begin buying stocks or bonds or investing in a mutual fund.

When you invest, there is a risk involved, but the primary point of investing is to make money. For the most part, your stocks will do that over a given period of time. In fact, the stock market has averaged more than 11 percent per year for the last seventy years. That means your money would have doubled in about six years. The stock market averages about one bad year in every four, so don't be discouraged if your investments experience a temporary drop. Remember, the stock market goes down temporarily, but up permanently. You also want to take an approach that diminishes the risk. One strategy that works is to create a solid portfolio of diversified investments.

Still not convinced that investing is for you? Well, consider this—you can't afford not to. With standard savings, your money will never generate the kind of money that long-term investment vehicles, such as stocks, bonds, and mutual funds, can. Inflation is always a factor when figuring the rate of return. With regular savings, your money may not be able to keep up with the cost of living whereas a stock could with compounded returns. This makes investment an attractive option.

BEFORE YOU INVEST

Before you invest, review your current financial condition. Are you still paying money on high-interest debt? Do you have your emergency savings (enough to live off three to six months) safely set aside? How strong is your budget plan? It doesn't make much sense to invest if other areas of your budget need to be taken care of first. After you pay off these areas, begin your investment program.

STOCKS

What are they? Stocks allow you to own pieces of a business. One stock symbolizes a proportional share of ownership in a company. If you own shares of Disney stock, you are part owner of Disneyland. Your share may be small, but you can tell your friends, "I'm an owner," the next time you visit Disneyland or Disney World. The value of the stock depends upon the value of the company, which generally follows a rise-and-fall cycle. There are two types of stock, common and preferred. Typically you'll be dealing with common stock. Understanding these investments should help you develop a mixed portfolio that will grow your investments.

COMMON STOCKS

Common stock is just that. Most investors own common stock simply because anyone can own it; there are no restrictions involved.

As a shareholder, you own part of a company and, therefore, part of the company's assets.

As part business owner, you are entitled to one vote (per each stock share). Thus, you can participate in board of director votes. You have a voice in determining who will oversee major company decisions because their decisions affect the value of your stock.

In case you're not familiar with how companies are operated, a board of directors determines how company money is spent and what investments the company will make to expand and strengthen the business.

When the company begins to grow, acquiring more assets and generating cash, the value of the company rises. A rise in the company value causes your stock value to increase. If the company earns substantial profits one year, your return will reflect this. If it has been a bad year for business, your return will reflect this. The board of directors may declare a dividend to be paid to shareholders. A dividend is a portion of the company's profits. You make money on stocks two ways: appreciation in value and dividends. This is called total return.

The worst case scenario occurs when a company goes bankrupt. Then your stock will be considered worthless. That is a risk involved with common stock investment. That also explains why a number of investors check to see how their stocks are doing, hoping to avoid a total loss.

Common stocks are often categorized as either growth or value stocks based on characteristics of the company.

GROWTH STOCKS

The stock of a company that reinvests the bulk of its profits to grow the business and aggressively expand its value is categorized as growth stock. The company will not pay much, if any, in dividends. Instead, people invest in such companies for the long term, hoping that as the value of the company grows, so will the value of their stock shares.

Value Stocks

Value stocks tend to be shares of older, established companies that no longer have rapid growth. These stocks usually pay the highest dividends because the company is no longer reinvesting as much profit in growing the company.

Preferred Stocks

When you purchase preferred stock, your dividends will be fixed. It's possible that you'll get money back even if the business folds. This may seem like a relatively safe bet. However, if the business really grows, your dividends often do not because they're fixed.

Penny Stocks

You've probably heard of penny stocks. These shares typically sell for $5 or less. There have been instances when penny stocks have gained significant value, but usually these stocks do not grow substantially and sometimes the business ends up folding. These are high-risk stocks, not for beginners.

Blue-Chip Stocks

Stocks of large, established companies that have a long-established track record and are consistently profitable are frequently called blue-chip stocks. Owning these shares is an investment for the long term. Investors may favor these stocks because their growth is steady and stable. It's possible the companies can lose this standing, however. You should track the progress of your stocks, although a drastic plummet of value is less likely with blue-chip stocks than with small company stocks. Examples of blue-chip stocks include Wal-Mart, General Motors, Coca-Cola, and McDonald's.

Defensive Stocks

Another way investors diminish their risk is to include a few shares of defensive stocks. Businesses such as utility companies, drug companies, health care companies, and other companies associated with consumer products that are in constant demand, in spite of the ups and downs of the economy, offer another means to generate steady returns. If the rest of the market experiences dramatic cycles, defensive stocks will remain fairly steady in value and thus minimize or offset the potentially volatile performances of higher-risk investments.

Cyclical Stocks

Cyclical stocks are the opposite of defensive stocks. Owning cyclical stock means you have shares in a business that traditionally performs well at certain times and less so at others. For example, travel industries undergo peak periods and then lose money when people cut back on expenses because of other market factors. Timing is the key to owning cyclical stocks. It's possible that if you purchase them before an upswing, you stand to make considerable earnings when the stocks peak. Selling at the right time is also critical.

HOW TO BUY STOCKS

Purchasing and tracking stocks require a fairly thorough understanding of how stocks are traded. It's even possible to benefit from purchasing stock options and futures, perhaps the riskiest stock ventures. However, I'm not going to discuss *how* to invest in this chapter. I'm simply explaining what stocks are and some of the advantages and disadvantages associated with certain types of stocks.

The most common method to purchase stock is through a brokerage firm. There are full-service brokers, such as Merrill Lynch and

Edward Jones; discount brokers, such as Charles Schwab; and deep discount brokers such as E*TRADE. Research brokerages carefully. Don't hand over your hard-earned money to just anybody. Many online services can help you evaluate a broker, and established brokerages are listed in your local directory.

The one aspect of working with a brokerage that you should know about is this: you will have either a cash account or a margin account. A cash account is self-explanatory. What is a margin account, though? A margin account loans you money to purchase stocks. A margin account enhances your buying power, which is something to be wary of or at the least very careful with. Brokers make a substantial portion of their earnings from margin loans, and margin purchases generate commissions. You may make money with a margin account, but you need to be aware that brokers may strongly encourage you to open a margin account. Only you can make this decision. Consider your entire financial picture, and seek out more than one opinion. Buying stocks involves risk. It's simply a matter of weighing the risk with the potential value of the return.

BONDS

Many investors find bonds attractive because they pay regular interest income. Bonds also come with a pledge to repay the bond amount. How do they differ from stocks? Bonds are loans. The borrower promises to repay the principal (original bond amount) when the bond matures (a fixed date) as well as pay interest (coupon rate). What are coupons? Most bonds have preset coupons that consistently pay fixed income to the investor.

Borrowers raise capital by issuing bonds to investors. Typically borrowers are the U.S. government, states, cities, corporations, and other institutions. Government bonds are attractive to many investors because they have investment security. The issuer may back the bond with "full faith and credit" to repay the bond.

Bonds are fixed-income investments, which means they make regular interest payments up until the date of maturity. If your bond has a long maturity period, you'll probably be offered higher interest rates to compensate for fluctuating interest rates that can affect the price of the bond.

The advantage of bonds? Generally they provide higher returns than cash investments. They also tend to perform ahead of inflation.

TYPES OF BONDS

There are different types of bonds, and they vary depending on the issuer, the maturity date, and the credit quality. The following is a partial list of available bonds:

- U.S. government securities
- Mortgage-backed Securities
- Municipal bonds
- Corporate bonds
- Junk bonds

Another factor that makes bonds an attractive investment option is that they usually pay income semiannually. Once you own bonds, keep an eye on interest rates. When interest rates rise, bond prices drop. It's typical for bond values to move in the opposite direction of interest rates.

U.S. GOVERNMENT SECURITIES

Treasury bonds are considered the safest investment in the world. Because the government can raise taxes to pay off its debts, chances are slim that your bond will be defaulted on. Interest earned is usually exempt from state and local taxes. Federal taxes, however, are another story.

These bonds tend to have intermediate (two to ten years) and long-term (ten to thirty years) maturity dates. They provide income for government-funded projects. You can purchase treasury bonds directly, unlike other bonds that require a broker, by using a federal system called Treasury Direct. You can visit the Web site at www.treasurydirect.gov.

MORTGAGE-BACKED SECURITIES

These bonds are purchased from secondary lenders, such as Fannie Mae and Freddie Mac, which resell existing mortgages. How does this work? Well, Fannie Mae will purchase a mortgage from a lender. Next, Fannie Mae will repackage the mortgage; it then becomes a security that is sold to investors.

MUNICIPAL BONDS

Sold by states, cities, and local governments, "munis" lend money directly to your community. Interest earned is exempt from federal taxes. Munis are also exempt from state and local taxes if you reside in the state where the bonds were issued. You will have to pay taxes on capital gains earned from your municipal bond.

CORPORATE BONDS

Used to raise capital, corporate bonds are generally issued conglomerates, financial services, industrial businesses, public utilities, and transportation industries. These types of bonds are riskier than government-issued bonds. Individual corporations back them, so you'll want to do investigative research before buying.

There are rating systems to help you determine the financial stability of a company offering bonds. Insured corporate bonds are AAA rated and are very safe. Although the risk is higher, the interest rate will also be higher. These bonds are subject to taxes.

JUNK BONDS

Companies that are experiencing financial trouble may offer junk bonds so that they can raise some cash. Or a company may offer bonds to avoid selling more shares of stock to raise money. Junk bonds will have low ratings or no ratings at all. Consequently junk bonds are very high-risk investments.

Again, because the risk is higher, the yields are higher to compensate. If you're really interested in purchasing junk bonds, you might want to consider a junk bond mutual fund. That way, your investment is spread out over a number of companies, diminishing your overall risk while offering you the potential to earn high-yield interest.

CAPITAL GAINS CONSIDERATIONS

Bond prices fluctuate, so it's quite possible that you could resell your bond at a higher price than what you originally paid for it. In this instance, you will have to pay capital gains on your profit margin. If you hold your bond for less than a year (twelve months), you are subject to a short-term capital gains rate. This rate is the same as your ordinary tax rate. On the other hand, a long-term capital gains rate is applied to bonds held longer than a year. This rate is generally 20 percent for most investors. If you're in the 15 percent tax bracket, your rate will be 10 percent.

MUTUAL FUNDS

Mutual funds are collections of stocks and/or bonds. Usually a professional mutual fund manager actively buys and sells the stocks and bonds the fund holds. Mutual funds generally have an objective providing the fund manager with direction. The fund itself represents a collective of investors who have pooled their money to take advantage of the higher-yield rates of stocks and bonds. Mutual funds can be a combination of the following: bonds, cash instruments, and stocks.

How does it work? You purchase shares in a mutual fund. Because the fund is owned collectively, your investment is already diversified and spread out over a number of securities. Some mutual funds may hold the stock of more than one hundred companies. This leverages your holdings, a scenario difficult to create as a single investor. All of the fund's earnings are shared among the investors.

ADVANTAGES

If you do not have the time or patience to carefully research or track your investments, a mutual fund provides you with professional money management. Stocks and bonds are already diversified, an excellent long-term investment strategy. Should you wish to cash out of your fund, you can do so at any time without having to actively find a buyer.

DISADVANTAGES

Professional money management appears to be a very attractive option. However, a large number of mutual funds actually underperform compared with an average stock market return. Management fees may also compromise mutual fund returns. Another factor to think about? Control. After all, someone else is picking your stocks.

Then there's dilution. Even though your fund has ownership in a large number of stocks, the percentage may be so small that when a stock performs very well, the yield is small. With a mutual fund, you're focusing on the total performance and not individual stocks.

Also keep your eye out for buried costs. Sales and management fees can be hidden within the fund's information, so use your discretion.

WRAP-UP

Investing may seem complicated. Take your time, and educate yourself on how the stock market works. Be patient. Right now, there's a tremendous amount of information for you to use to find your way to greater financial security.

Seek the advice of experts and friends. Maybe take a course or consult one of the many online financial sites to enhance your understanding. Yes, the market can be risky. However, in the long run, investments will grow your wealth and give you a higher return rate than a standard savings account, money market account, or CD.

Because you're trying to build your wealth, it pays to get involved with investments. Stocks have historically outperformed other long-term investment vehicles, giving you the highest return for your money. That may be a good place for you to start.

Visit my Web site at *www.financialvictory.com* for a referral to a Financial Adviser or financial planner in your area.

COACH'S TIP

Your confidence will grow the more you learn about investing strategies, as will your personal wealth if you grow it carefully and wisely.

22

GIVING AND RECEIVING

———

Learning how to give is just as important as learning how to receive. There is a proverb that says, "A generous man will prosper; he who refreshes others will himself be refreshed" (Prov.11:25 NIV). What truth in those words!

Being in a position to give money, whether you have a lot or very little, to help someone in need, to contribute to your church or place of worship, a charitable organization, or another needy cause will open you up to receive blessings in your life.

These blessings may not be returned as money. Blessings could be good health, a loving family, the knowledge that you have helped someone in need, and delight in watching your church or place of worship spread money to help others or even add to its own building program. Simply realizing that your money was used to further medical research and a charitable cause can be blessing enough.

The needs in this world are immense. Without financial support from women like you and me, many medical and charitable breakthroughs might not have happened. Lives might not have been touched without you reaching out to give generously with no thought of receiving something in return.

There are times when you may have little but manage to give what you can. Don't overlook such seemingly small acts of kindness. No gift is ever really too small. When you share what you have, a blessing comes back to you. Those who have even less than you and receive your gift see only your generous spirit. How do I know this for certain? Let me share a story with you.

A CHRISTMAS STORY

Many years ago, when my three daughters were grade-school age, we were faced with some financial challenges. It was Christmas time, and I began to think of what I had been thankful for during that year, which was the good health of my family.

We had experienced some turbulent years and had been plagued by constant health problems of one kind or another. So one year of good health really made me realize what a blessing that was. I thought, *What can I do to help someone else in need?*

I contacted our county hospital to see if there were any children who would be in the hospital over the Christmas holiday. A case-worker told me that eight terminally ill children would be in the hospital during that time. She gave me their ages and gracefully indicated that one child had a family in great need.

I had only $100 to work with; it was all I could afford. I needed to be creative with that amount of money, so my family pitched in to help. Our project? To get presents to those children before Christmas Eve.

My three daughters and I watched the newspapers daily for sales. We began shopping, and I watched as my daughters' enthusiasm for the project grew. Shortly thereafter, each said to me, "Mom and Dad, don't buy us any Christmas presents this year. Use the money to buy more presents for the needy children."

Well, when we finished shopping, my family and I spent the

evening individually wrapping the gifts. We also bought a gift certificate for groceries for the family in need. I don't know how we did it, but that $100 went a long way, and each child received more than one gift.

The next morning, I watched as my husband, Hal, and the girls placed the presents in a large green trash bag. Hal slung the trash bag over his shoulder like Santa Claus, and headed over to the hospital to deliver the gifts. It's a sight I'll never forget.

On Christmas Day my daughters opened their presents. At different times, one of them would stop and say, "I wonder how the children liked their gifts?" It was truly a memorable Christmas and a wonderful blessing for each of us.

The blessing didn't end that day. Two weeks after Christmas, we received a check in the mail. It was for $100! It was from an overpayment to our insurance company. I had no idea that we were owed any money. That check was completely unexpected.

It's my belief that we were all created to help others in our lives. You might say to yourself, *I don't have much, so how can I give money away?* Well, if you don't have money, you have time. Give your time to your church or place of worship or a charity. That is giving. Your time is worth money. And when you have it, give money when you can.

FINDING EXTRA MONEY TO GIVE

To help you find money or set some aside to give, avoid instances of wasted spending. If you have change that you toss in a box, count it at the end of each month, and give it away. You'll be surprised at how that spare change can add up.

I know when our money was plentiful, I was able to give more money to helping others. Yet when we hit a financial slump and had little money, we were still blessed by others.

Most people never knew about our financial problems. There were times when we had to turn down dinner invitations because of our finances. Then out of nowhere, the other couple would say, "We want you to be our guests for dinner."

Another time, I tagged along with my sister Cathy while she shopped. At one point Cathy turned to me and said, "This dress would look great on you. I want to get it for you." When you don't have money for these sorts of things, you really see the blessings behind such generosity.

GIVING MONTHLY

At the beginning of every month allocate how much you want to give. A common amount to set aside is 10 percent of your income. If you can't handle that much, allocate what you can. Something is better than nothing.

Next, write out your check at the beginning of each month to the organization or person that you want to donate to. That way it's always in your mind, and you've formed a good habit. If that doesn't work for you, write out the check when you can.

TAX DEDUCTIBLE GIFTS

For a gift to be considered tax deductible, you must donate to a qualified organization. Religious, charitable, educational, artistic, scientific, and literary organizations generally adhere to federal requirements, allowing them to be recognized as qualified. Organizations that meet federal requirements will have 501(c)(3) status. You can contact the IRS for a publication that lists qualified organizations. If you donate to any 501(c)(3) organization, you'll receive a receipt or annual summary of your giving that can be deducted on your tax return.

You are not limited to cash donations. You can reduce your taxes by donating appreciated stocks. Depending upon the amount donated and your tax bracket, you could save money on your taxes.

If you're making estate plans and want to avoid passing on high taxes to your heirs, a lifetime donation can help you achieve this goal. You may want to speak with an estate expert.

For those whose donations may be smaller, don't feel that they don't make a difference. On average, most Americans give about 2 percent of their income (before taxes), which translates to an estimated $1,075 per average household, which equals $3 a day! Some statistics show households whose income is under $10,000 give up to 5.2 percent of their income. If they can come up with the money, so can you.

CARS, FURNITURE, AND OTHER TANGIBLE PIECES OF PROPERTY

You can get a tax deduction for donating items such as cars, books, appliances, and other such goods to a charitable organization. There are different rules for certain types of gifts, but in general, if you give an item such as a car to an organization, the deduction will be treated like short-term property. The deduction amount will be based on what you paid for it or its current market value. But keep in mind that you gain by helping out a worthy cause.

TIPS ON GIVING

If you want to receive a tax deduction for a donation, make sure the organization you've selected has a 501(c)(3) IRS classification. Such an organization has been given tax-exempt status, which means it can accept contributions. Not all nonprofits qualify for this status, so if you give them a donation, you may not qualify for a tax deduction. Check with the IRS for a listing of 501(c)(3) charities.

Keep such information on hand in the event that you're audited; make a note of the organization's name, the donation amount, and the date of the contribution. If you pay your donation by check, credit card, or e-mail, keep this paperwork along with the appropriate information noted somewhere on it. For anything other than a cash donation, you'll also need written acknowledgment from the charity listing the property received along with an estimate of the value. File this paperwork; you'll need to include it with your tax return.

GIVING WISELY

Use wisdom before giving. Many organizations need your gifts. But there are also a lot of scam operations. How do you avoid giving to a disreputable organization? Always ask for written information. Legitimate charities will provide you with materials explaining who they are and what their mission is. They'll include information on how the money is used and can give you a receipt to prove that your donation is tax deductible.

Be careful of names that sound right but may be slightly off. Sometimes scam organizations use a name that sounds like a legitimate charity. If you have any doubts, call the charity in question. Ask if the administrators are aware of the solicitation and know that the charity's name is being used to generate donations. If they're not, someone operating under false pretenses may have approached you.

Never allow high-pressure tactics to force you into making a donation. Most legitimate organizations will not submit you to such tactics, because they're interested in having you become a loyal donor and giving what you can when you have it to give.

Be cautious when you receive free merchandise for a contribution. These items are paid for out of donations just like yours. Do you want your money used in this way, or do you want it used for the charity? The choice is up to you. Pay by check or credit card; that way you have an accurate record of the donation, and it's safer than paying with cash.

GIVING FROM THE HEART, NOT FOR A DEDUCTION

Many times you will be moved to give from the heart for an immediate cause or person in need and not receive a tax deduction. You don't want to have the attitude of giving only for receiving. If you do that, you have the wrong attitude. Regard giving as an extension of your time or money to see how it makes a difference.

A person or organization may come to your mind that you feel needs financial help. That may be the time you need to give without knowing the reason why. Something like that occurred when I started my own business. When I received my first order, I had a strong urge to send that money to a friend of ours who was working overseas as a missionary. Without knowing why, I mailed the check.

I hadn't spoken to my friend for several years, but I sent the check anyway. A couple of years later when she was back in town, she came to our home and visited. She indicated that the day she received the check, she had picked up the mail and headed off to a dental appointment without opening the letter. She had to have dental work done and didn't know how she was going to pay for it. As she waited in the dentist office, she opened the letter, and there was the check. She couldn't believe her eyes. It was enough to pay for all the dental work. She was blessed, and years later when I heard the story, I was blessed too.

WRAP-UP

Giving can be a wonderful way to feel good about your prosperity and the many blessings you receive in this life. Most of us are quite fortunate and are capable of sharing some of that fortune with others. There's a saying that what you give, you receive. I believe this to be true. When you give and know that it's needed and appreciated, the feeling it gives you is priceless. Remember that it is the collected efforts of individuals, like you and me, that make the difference for all kinds of people and causes in need.

COACH'S TIP

Don't wait for a needy cause to fall in your lap. Look for a cause, and do something about it.

Conclusion

ACHIEVING FINANCIAL SECURITY

———

Nothing is more gratifying than winning a game or arriving at the destination you carefully mapped out to reach.

During your financial journey, you stretched a little, had a vigorous workout, planned and plotted how you would become a financially secure woman. With time on your side, knowledge in your head, and excitement in your heart, there is no reason you won't succeed.

You may experience pitfalls along the way, but pick yourself right back up, brush off the dust, and keep moving. You can do it! I'm rooting for you! Progress may be slow, but you will build up speed to reach the finish line and gain the financial victory you deserve.

A wise proverb proclaims: "Plans fail for lack of counsel, but with many advisers they succeed" (Prov. 15:22 NIV).

I encourage you to seek the advice of experts in the areas of your concerns. Read books; attend financial and credit seminars to gain knowledge; ask questions. If you don't know the answers, visit my Web site at *www.FinancialyVictory.com* for a referrel list of experts and any questions you may have.

Remember, knowledge brings power. Now go win that race!

ABOUT THE AUTHOR

DEBORAH McNAUGHTON is the founder of Professional Credit Counselors. She is a nationally known credit expert and financial coach who has been interviewed on hundreds of radio and television talk shows talking about credit, mortgages, real estate and automobile purchases, and financial planning.

She is the author of several books on credit including, *Destroy Your Debt: Your Guide to Financial Freedom, All About Credit: Questions and Answers to the Most Common Credit Problems, The Insiders Guide to Managing Your Credit, Everything You Need to Know about Credit, Fix Your Credit, Have a Good Credit Report* (coauthored with John Avanzini), and *The Credit Repair System,* a business opportunity manual that has helped hundreds of credit counseling businesses throughout the United States get started. McNaughton conducts credit and financial strategies seminars nationally and publishes a monthly newsletter titled "Financial Victory." She also has a video and workbook seminar series called "Your Financial Future: Understanding Credit, Debt, and Planning for Tomorrow."

In 1990, McNaughton founded Inner-Strength International, introducing her motivational workshop and manual "Yes You Can" to help individuals discover their full potential in life by focusing on finances, hope, and encouragement.

To receive more information about McNaughton's seminars, referrals, products, and services, write:

> Deborah McNaughton
> 1100 Irvine Boulevard #541
> Tustin, CA 92780
> Or call:
> 714-541-2637

If you have any comments or questions, visit her website at:
Financialvictory.com

ACKNOWLEDGMENTS

One of the greatest challenges in life is to be able to share your vision with someone and watch them take hold of it. I want to take a moment to introduce my collaborator Carla Gentry. It was Carla's, encouragement, enthusiasm and hours of hard work that helped me complete this project. Carla, you're the greatest.

A special thanks to the team at Thomas Nelson, especially my editor, Victor Oliver, for keeping me focused and expanding my horizons. Also Kristen Lucas, my managing editor, for keeping things moving in the right direction.

To my agent, Chip MacGregor, who constantly makes me laugh and is there to bounce new ideas and projects off of. I know I can count on Chip to help me make the right decisions.

I want to thank the team at Cambridge Credit Counseling Corp., where I am a spokesperson. Thank you for your wealth of information and for helping people. John Puccio, Chris Viale, and Thom Fox. You're the greatest. Keep up the good work.

For my family. How can I express my gratitude to my husband, daughters, sons-in-laws and grand-children who patiently waited for me to emerge from this project and once again call me wife, mom and nana? The best I can do is say I love you all.

A special thank you to the women who have been brave enough to tackle money issues and share their stories with me as well as tell me what they need to know about their finances.

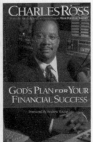
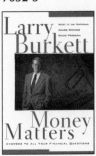
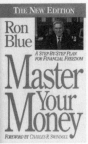